LOW-GI
VEGETARIAN
COOKBOOK

LOW-GI VEGETARIAN COOKBOOK

ROSE ELLIOT

BOOKS

Food photography by Michael Paul

So many people have been involved with this book in one way or another and I would like to thank them all: Viv Bowler, Senior Commissioning Editor at BBC Worldwide, and my agent, Barbara Levy, for seeing and sharing my vision for the book and helping to make it a reality, for which the talents of Isobel Gillan, designer, and Michael Paul, photographer, were essential, and much appreciated and valued. The photographic shoots were a particular pleasure – I'd like to thank Louise Mackaness for preparing the food so well, Kumiko Ochiai for styling the shots (as well as making wonderful coffee and giving me tips on Japanese cooking), and Yuki Sugiura for helping at the shoots. A big thank you, too, to Sarah Reece, who not only kept everything running smoothly throughout the editorial process, but also posed for all the chapter-opener shots. You're a star, Sarah. I'd also like to thank Rachel Connolly for her thorough yet sensitive editing of the text; Mari Roberts, brilliant editor of the new GI edition; Kelly Davis for proofreading; Hilary Bird for indexing; Dr Jacqueline Stordy for information on omega-3 oils; Lyndel Costain for advice on nutrition, and the Vegetarian Society for general information and advice. As ever, a huge thank you to my family and friends, who must feel as if they have lived with this book for months, and most of all to my husband, Robert, who really has, helping with shopping, tasting, washing up and being generally patient and supportive. Thank you Robert, thank you everyone. It was really appreciated.

5 7 9 10 8 6 4

Published in 2007 by BBC Books, an imprint of Ebury Publishing
Originally published in hardback as *Fast, Fresh and Fabulous* in 2003
Ebury Publishing is a division of the Random House Group

The Random House Group Limited Reg. No. 954009

Addresses for companies within the Random House Group can be found at www.randomhouse.co.uk

A CIP catalogue record for this book is available from the British Library

The Random House Group Limited makes every effort to ensure that the papers used in our
books are made from trees that have been legally sourced from well-managed and credibly certified forests.
Our paper procurement policy can be found on www.randomhouse.co.uk

ISBN 978 0 563 53921 6

Commissioning editor: Vivien Bowler   Project editors: Sarah Reece and Mari Roberts
Copy-editor: Rachel Connolly   Art director: Sarah Ponder   Designer: Isobel Gillan   Stylist: Kumiko
Home economist: Louise Mackaness   Production controllers: Christopher Tinker and Peter Hunt

Set in GillSans
Printed and bound by Firmengruppe APPL, aprinta druck, Wemding, Germany
Colour separations by Radstock Reproductions Ltd, Midsomer Norton

CONTENTS

ABOUT THIS BOOK

THE GI – GLYCAEMIC INDEX – HAS FASCINATED ME EVER SINCE I FIRST READ ABOUT IT AND

REALIZED THAT EATING LOW-GI FOODS IS A FABULOUS WAY TO GET SLIM AND STAY SLIM.

Eating low-GI foods is a way to be slim while eating delicious, healthy, 'normal' food, without calorie-counting or even serious limiting of portions. For a health-conscious food-lover who is also vain enough to want to be thin, this really seemed to be the answer …

So I used the GI in my own cooking and based my book *Fast, Fresh and Fabulous* on it. This was done in a low-key way because at the time the term 'GI' was still very much 'dietician speak'. How times change: now 'GI' is everywhere! So we decided to call this beautiful new edition the *Low-GI Vegetarian Cookbook*, and I have greatly expanded upon the glycaemic index, describing in detail how to use it for effective, permanent weight loss, and for good health and vitality at every stage of life.

What exactly, then, is the GI, and what's so good about it? The 'GI' is the glycaemic index, which is a measure of how food affects our blood glucose. Any food containing carbohydrate registers on the GI according to how quickly it raises our blood glucose – our 'blood sugar' level – as it is broken down and digested.

This is important, because while we need carbohydrates for energy, we don't need the 'wrong' sort: those with a high rating on the GI index. These are converted rapidly into glucose in the body, giving us the familiar 'sugar high'. Too much glucose in the bloodstream can be harmful and has to be removed rapidly. To do this, the body takes emergency action: it releases high levels of insulin, which remove glucose from the blood into the cells, where it is used as energy and any excess stored or converted to fat.

Then, an hour or so after eating a high-GI food, we get an energy 'low' and the desire for another quick energy fix – and, if we eat more of the 'wrong' carbohydrates at this point, the cycle continues. This distorts our natural appetite, making us crave snacks because we never feel satisfied. If this process is repeated too often, we may become 'insulin resistant', which means it takes ever larger amounts of insulin to reduce our blood sugar. This can lead to high blood pressure, diabetes, raised cholesterol and the increased storage of fat – a group of symptoms known as metabolic syndrome, or Syndrome X.

What we need is low-GI carbohydrates, from which the glucose is released slowly and steadily. These carbohydrates keep us feeling full and satisfied for longer. The body has time to use the glucose methodically, which gives us a sustained, steady flow of energy.

Eating these healthy carbohydrates can have a positive effect on every part of your body, from the digestive system to the heart and even the skin. A low-GI diet has been shown not only to help achieve and maintain a healthy weight, but also to reduce the risk of stroke, prevent or control diabetes and possibly even reduce the risk of breast cancer and Alzheimer's disease. It is a very healthy way of eating and perfectly suited to the vegetarian and vegan way of life.

In the following pages I've explained how to eat a healthy vegetarian or vegan diet, whatever your age and situation. You'll find details of the proteins you need, as well as the low-GI carbohydrates, and how you can make sure you're getting the necessary minerals, vitamins and essential fats. Plus, how to plan balanced meals, and how you can use the GI to lose weight, gain health and never have to diet again.

★ These are the best recipes for slimming. Eat as much of these as you like.

COOK'S NOTES

The ingredients you need are fully described and explained throughout the book and there is also a list of stockists at the back (see page 192), so I hope you'll find everything clear and easy to follow. Many of the ingredients are easy to get just about anywhere; a few are less well known and available in health-food shops and specialist supermarkets, although they are beginning to creep onto the shelves of ordinary supermarkets.

All the recipes in this book list both imperial and metric measurements. Conversions are approximate and have been rounded up or down. In most of the recipes you can be fairly relaxed about measuring but to be on the safe side it's always best to choose one set of measurements and stick with it, rather than mixing them.

If you have a fan oven, you need to reduce the temperatures given throughout this book, as recommended by your oven manufacturer. On my oven this usually means reducing the heat by about two notches on the dial, so 180°C/350°F becomes 160°C/325°F, and so on.

When eggs are used, they are medium ('large' in the US), free-range and preferably organic.

Australian cooks

Your tablespoons measure 20 ml (4 teaspoons) whereas ours are only 15 ml (3 teaspoons), so where tablespoons are given, please measure 3 teaspoons to get the correct amount.

American cooks

Your pints are smaller – only 450 ml whereas ours are 600 ml. So for liquids please use a British pint measure or follow the metric quantities given.

A HEALTHY VEGETARIAN OR VEGAN LOW-GI DIET IS ONE

THAT PROVIDES ALL THE NUTRIENTS WE NEED FOR ENERGY, GROWTH, REPAIR, MAINTENANCE AND PROTECTION, IN ROUGHLY THE RIGHT PROPORTIONS. WE NEED PROTEIN, CARBOHYDRATES, VITAMINS, MINERALS AND ESSENTIAL FATS – AND A LOW-GI VEGETARIAN OR VEGAN DIET CAN SUPPLY THEM ALL.

PROTEIN

Protein is essential for growth, maintenance and repair of tissues, and for the healthy functioning of the body. The best sources of protein are:

- nuts and seeds
- beans and lentils
- soya milk and yogurt
- natural protein foods such as tofu, tempeh and seitan
- new protein products such as TVP and Quorn
- dairy food, including milk, cheese and yogurt
- free-range eggs

There is also protein in grains and cereals, especially quinoa, though they are mainly carbohydrate (see pages 114–115). Many foods, even potatoes, apples and leafy vegetables, contain small amounts of protein.

All protein, whether of animal or vegetable origin, is made up of building-blocks called amino acids, arranged in different patterns in different foods. When your body has unpicked the patterns it doesn't know whether these blocks have come from chickens, chick peas or chicory.

There are twenty of these amino acids. Our bodies can make some of them, but there are nine which it cannot. These are called essential amino acids. Like meat and fish, all the protein foods mentioned above contain these essential amino acids, but the mix in animal proteins is

closer to what our bodies want. The vegetable proteins are a bit more erratic; however the great thing is that the amino acids some lack, others can supply. Grains are rich in one of the essential amino acids, beans in another, so if you have, say, baked beans on toast, hummus and pitta bread, or lentil dal and rice, you are getting the full complement. This mixing often happens naturally in a meal, but if it doesn't, your body can store unused amino acids for matching up later.

You can get all the protein you need from vegetable sources. The trick is to eat as wide a variety of these foods as possible and to resist the temptation to rely too much on dairy foods. That way you get the benefit of maximum nourishment and optimum health.

CARBOHYDRATE

Carbohydrate is our main source of energy, and is found in three forms:

- simple sugars, found in fruit, milk and all types of sugar
- complex carbohydrates or starches, found in cereals and grains such as bread, rice, potatoes and all vegetables. Beans and lentils contain complex carbohydrate as well as protein.
- fibre, now called non-starch polysaccharide (NSP), is the cellulose, tough cell walls and gums in fruits, vegetables and cereals. It's indigestible but vital to the healthy functioning of the gut.

As I've explained on pages 6–7, our bodies break carbohydrates down into simple sugars, which are then absorbed into our bloodstream, giving us energy. Generally, the more fibrous a carbohydrate, the more slowly it is broken down as the sugars are separated from the fibre during digestion, and the lower its rating on the GI. This gives slow, sustained energy and is one of the reasons why complex carbohydrates such as whole grains, vegetables and pulses are so beneficial. Processed cereals, potatoes, white bread, cakes, sugary drinks and snacks, refined sugar and products made from it all have a high GI rating and go relatively quickly into our bloodstream, giving a quick energy lift, which is less sustained and means we may soon be looking for another boost.

The glycaemic index

Foods with little or no carbohydrate, such as oils and fats, meat, fish and cheese don't have a GI rating. Any food containing carbohydrate (starches and sugars), however, does register on the glycaemic index, according to how quickly it raises your blood glucose (sugar) level as it is broken down and digested. The more refined, sweet and starchy the food, the higher it registers on the GI. It gives you a quick energy-burst but stresses your system to release insulin rapidly and quickly store or use the blood glucose.

Most fruits are low on the index, with the exception of very sweet, tropical varieties: pineapple, also melons and watermelon. Sugary and refined foods are high, while beans and lentils are low, as are many whole grains including oats, barley, buckwheat and quinoa. Most rice is high, though basmati rice, both brown and white, is only medium, especially if cooked al dente.

Raw vegetables and most cooked vegetables are low, but mashed potato is high – in general, potatoes are lower when they're new, unpeeled and slightly undercooked or baked and eaten with their skins, but they're still on the high side and best eaten with lots of raw vegetables to slow up the absorption of the sugars.

It's healthiest to eat foods with a low or medium GI but you don't need complicated reference books and calculators – most of the time this means sticking to whole, unrefined cereals, pulses, tofu, vegetables and fruit. If you do eat foods with a high GI, you can lessen the effect by eating them with something with a low rating, such as yogurt, pulses, fruit or vegetables.

Fat also slows the digestion of carbohydrates, and so lowers the GI rating of a food, which is why croissants have a medium rating while white bread is high. Obviously adding lashings of fat to a meal is not the answer, especially if you want to lose weight, but including some healthy oil – a lightly dressed salad, for instance – is a good way of lowering the GI rating of a meal.

Adding fresh lemon juice (or vinegar) also significantly lowers the GI rating of a food; the reasons are not clear, but it may have something to do with the acidic qualities of the lemon juice, which is great, because a dash of lemon juice enhances the flavour of so many foods as well as providing vitamin C and other body-protecting antioxidants.

THE GI FOOD TABLE

This table shows the low, medium and high GI ratings of common vegetarian and vegan foods.
* Limit portion while slimming, see opposite.

Foods with Low GI

FRUITS

Most, including:

Apples, fresh and dried

Apricots, fresh and dried

Avocado*

Bananas

Berries, frozen
  (without sugar)

Cherries

Figs, fresh

Grapefruit

Grapes

Kiwi fruit

Mangoes

Oranges and Mandarins

Peaches

Pears

Plums

Prunes

Satsumas

Strawberries

Sultanas

VEGETABLES

Most, including:

Alfalfa sprouts

Asparagus

Aubergine

Beans, green and runner

Beetroot (raw)

Broccoli

Brussels sprouts

Cabbage

Carrots (raw and cooked)

Cauliflower

Celery

Courgettes

Cucumber

Lettuce

Mangetout

Mushrooms

Okra

Olives

Onions

Pak choy (bok choy)

Parsley

Peas

Peppers

Potatoes (baby new only)*

Spring greens

Spring onions

Sweetcorn fresh, frozen or
  canned without sugar

Swiss chard

Spinach

Tomatoes

PULSES

Most dried beans and
  lentils

Canned beans and lentils
  without added sugar

Canned baked beans
  (no sugar)

Canned bean, lentil and
  chunky vegetable soups

Soya 'nuts', bought or
  home-made

BREADS AND CRISPBREADS*

100% stone-ground
  wholemeal bread

Wholegrain, high-fibre
  breads with 2½ to 3 g
  fibre per slice

High-fibre crispbreads

BREAKFAST CEREALS*

All-Bran

Bran

Traditional porridge oats

Oat bran

Homemade muesli

GRAINS*

Barley

Bulgar

Buckwheat

Oatmeal

Quinoa

PASTA*

Pasta – all types made
  from durum wheat

Buckwheat noodles

Noodles made from mung
  beans

NUTS AND SEEDS*

Almonds

Cashews

Flax or linseeds

Hazelnuts

Macadamia nuts

Peanuts

Peanut butter (no palm oil
  or added sugar)

Pistachios

Pumpkin seeds

Sesame seeds

Sunflower seeds

DRINKS AND SNACK FOODS

Chocolate drink: 'light',
  instant

Coffee, decaffeinated
  (without sugar)

Corn thins

Milk, skimmed

Popcorn, homemade, with
  olive oil and salt

Soya milk, unsweetened

Soya nuts

Soya-nut butter (a good
  alternative to peanut
  butter)

Tea, regular and herb
  (without sugar)

SWEETENERS

Apple juice concentrate

Stevia (page 164)

Foods with Medium GI

FRUITS
Figs, dried
Fruit spreads: extra fruit, low sugar
Raisins

VEGETABLES
Beetroots, cooked
Carrots, cooked
Potatoes, peeled and boiled
Sweet potatoes

BREADS
Crispbread with fibre
Croissants
Wholegrain breads
Wholemeal pitta bread

BREAKFAST CEREALS
Alpen Crunchy Bran
Shredded Wheat

GRAINS
Rice: basmati, white and brown; long-grain brown; wild*
Wheat berries

SWEETENERS
Agave syrup
Fructose
Honey: raw organic

Foods with High GI

FRUITS
Canned fruit in syrup
Cantaloupe melon
Dates
Honeydew melon
Watermelon

VEGETABLES
Broad beans
Baked potatoes
French fries
Mashed potatoes
Parsnips
Pumpkins
Swede

BREADS
Bagels
Baguettes
Bread, white or brown
Crispbreads

BREAKFAST CEREALS
Granola
Commercial muesli
Popcorn (sweetened)

GRAINS
Couscous
Millet
Polenta
Rice: short-grain white, instant
Millet

PASTA
All tinned pastas
Gnocchi

SNACK FOODS AND DRINKS
Alcoholic drinks
Biscuits
Chocolate and sweets
Cookies
Crisps
Doughnuts
Fruit drinks
Ice cream
Juice, sweetened
Milk, whole
Popcorn, sweetened
Pretzels
Rice cakes
Soft drinks, regular
Tortilla chips

SUGAR AND SWEETENERS
Corn syrup
Glucose
Sugar: all types

Low GI Portions

Many of the low-GI foods can be eaten freely, although some, because of the amount of fat or type of starch they contain, need to be eaten in a limited amount for most effective slimming. These foods are marked*; for slimming, size the portions as follows:

Avocado ¼

Bread, 2–3g fibre per slice
 1 slice

Crispbreads (high fibre)
 2 slices

Low-GI cereals
 60 g (2 oz)

Nuts
 avoid while slimming

Pasta
 40 g (1½ oz) dry weight

Potatoes, boiled, baby new
 2–3 (100 g)

Rice: basmati,
 brown or white
 50 g (1¾ oz) dry weight

MINERALS AND VITAMINS

Most minerals and vitamins pose no problems for vegetarians or vegans. A vegetarian or vegan diet, particularly the low-GI version, is typically richer in vitamins A and C, B vitamins biotin, panto-thenic acid, folate and B6, and magnesium, than a meat diet. We do need to look at iron, calcium, vitamin B12, vitamin D, riboflavin (B2) and iodine.

Iron

We need iron for healthy blood and energy, and since meat is a prime source, people often worry about how vegetarians and vegans can get enough. However, perhaps surprisingly, studies have consistently shown that vegetarians and vegans are no more likely to suffer from lack of iron than meat eaters. The following are good sources of iron:

- grains and grain products such as wholewheat bread and pasta, millet, quinoa

- fortified breakfast cereals
- dried fruit, especially apricots, figs and peaches
- nuts and seeds, especially almonds, pistachio nuts and pumpkin seeds
- lentils, peas and beans, including soya products
- molasses
- green leafy vegetables

A vital point is that we absorb more iron when we eat foods containing it alongside a good source of vitamin C, like lemon juice, fresh fruit, or vegetable juices. A balanced vegetarian or vegan diet, planned along the lines suggested in this book, includes sufficient iron.

Calcium

Calcium is essential for healthy bones and teeth. Most people know it's found in dairy produce, but there are also some rich vegetable sources. One cup of cooked kale contains about the same amount of usable calcium as a 175 ml (6 fl oz) glass of milk. Calcium is found in:

- milk, yogurt and cheese
- leafy green vegetables, such as purple sprouting broccoli, kale and watercress
- dried fruit, especially figs
- fortified soya milk, and tofu prepared with calcium sulphate – check the label
- blackstrap molasses
- tap water in hard water areas and some bottled mineral waters – read the label

The calcium issue is a complex one because a number of factors can affect our ability to absorb and retain it. As calcium is needed by the body to process protein, some apparently rich sources of calcium aren't that effective if they're also high in protein. That's one of the reasons why I think it's a mistake for vegetarians to rely too much on dairy products. It's important to eat other good sources of calcium, as listed above, regularly. And for vegans, these are essential and need to be eaten daily.

Healthy bones depend on other things as well as calcium. Vitamin D is essential for the proper absorption of calcium (see below) and so is magnesium, which is a constituent of chlorophyll and therefore abundant in green leafy vegetables – if you eat kale or watercress, you get both calcium and magnesium. Other good sources of magnesium are wholegrains, wheat germ, molasses, seeds, nuts, apples and figs. And don't forget that weight-bearing exercise, such as walking, running, dancing (though not swimming), is also important for building and keeping healthy bones.

We also need to reduce the amount of calcium our bodies lose. Cutting down on caffeine and alcohol can definitely help here, as can eating foods that contain the trace mineral boron – apples, grapes, pears, prunes, dates, raisins, almonds, peanuts and hazelnuts.

Vitamin B12

This is a vital vitamin, but only very tiny amounts are needed. Vegetarians can get this from dairy foods and free-range eggs. If you're a vegan, you just need to make sure that, preferably daily, you eat foods such as soya milk, yeast extract, veggie burgers or breakfast cereals that have been fortified with B12 (read the label). Alternatively, you can always take a supplement.

Vitamin D

Vitamin D is made by the action of the sun on our skin. It's also in milk, cheese and butter and is added to most margarines, including soya varieties.

Healthy adult vegetarians and vegans can usually get enough from these sources, but the very young, the very old and those who spend most of their time inside would be well advised to take a vitamin D supplement, especially if they're eating little or no dairy produce or margarine.

Riboflavin (B2)

We need this for the release of energy from food and for healthy skin, eyes and hair. For most people, milk and cheese are important sources of riboflavin, so vegans and vegetarians eating little dairy produce need to make sure they include other good sources, such as:

- almonds
- yeast and yeast extracts
- wheat germ and quinoa
- soya beans
- avocado
- fortified breakfast cereals
- soya milk

Iodine

We need iodine for the healthy functioning of the thyroid gland. Most people in the UK, including vegetarians, get about half their daily iodine from dairy products. Vegans and vegetarians eating only a little dairy produce can add iodine to their diet by eating some seaweed two or three times a week (see page 124). You don't need much iodine, and it's important not to over-do it – 115 g (4 oz) dried hijiki or 15g (½ oz) dried kombu provides a year's supply for one person. Nori doesn't contain much iodine and you can eat several sheets a day without worrying about overdosing. Using an unrefined salt will supply a balanced source of iodine as well as some trace minerals lacking in other salts.

ESSENTIAL FATS

All fats are made up of fatty acids, and these may be saturated like coconut oil, butter and animal fats, monounsaturated like olive oil, or polyunsaturated like sunflower, safflower and soya oil. Our bodies can make saturated and monounsaturated fats, but they can't make two polyunsaturated fats (PUFAs), linoleic acid and alpha-linolenic acid, parents of the omega-6 and omega-3 oils. So these are called essential fatty acids and they have to be provided by our food.

Linoleic acid and omega-6 oils are found in vegetables, fruits, nuts, grains and seeds; oils made from corn, sunflowers, soya, evening primrose, pumpkin and wheat germ are also good sources.

Alpha-linolenic acid and omega-3 oils are found in fish oils, eggs and blue-green algae, which presumably is where the fish get it from originally. These are called 'long chain' omega-3 oils. 'Short chain' omega-3 oils are found in flaxseeds, linseeds, walnuts, soya beans, rapeseed (canola) oils, leafy

green vegetables, grains, an algae called spirulina, and nori seaweed. You can also buy eggs which have been enriched with omega-3 by feeding the hens a supplement made from seeds or algae. Some of the vegetable sources of omega-3 are very rich: flaxseed oil, for instance, contributes twice as much omega-3 as fish oil, but it's not clear how efficiently our bodies can convert the short chain omega-3s into the long chain ones it needs.

This fat question is quite complex because it's not just our intake of the different fats but the proportions which are important. For instance, if we eat a lot of saturated fat (in milk, cheese, cream and eggs) we may impair our body's ability to process omega-6 and omega-3 oils, another reason for not over-doing the dairy. In addition, our utilization of omega-3 may be hindered if we have too high a level of omega-6. Because of all these factors, we now have a much higher proportion of omega-6 to omega-3 acids in our bodies than ever before. Some nutritional therapists are worried about this and attribute to it all kinds of aches and pains (such as the pre-menstrual syndrome) and even link it with cancer.

Studies have shown that vegetarians and vegans take in considerably more omega-6 than do omnivores, and roughly the same levels of omega-3. So in spite of the perceived healthiness of sunflower oil, vegetarians and vegans can achieve a better balance by using more omega-3 oils – rapeseed oil instead of sunflower, safflower or corn oil; walnut oil or cold-pressed rapeseed oil on salads as a change from olive oil; and a daily tablespoon of cold-pressed flaxseed oil or a rounded tablespoon of finely ground flaxseeds. To be on the safe side, I also recommend a daily supplement of algae-derived omega-3 oils such as Neuromins (see page 192).

TRANS FATTY ACIDS

Trans fatty acids are formed when unsaturated fats, such as vegetable oils, are hydrogenated to make them more solid, as in margarine and cooking fats. They are thus present in most bought cakes, biscuits, pastries, fried foods, and in many ready-meals and hard margarines. Trans fats are of concern because they may interfere with the body's ability to utilize omega-3 oils, which research is demonstrating are important for brain function, healthy blood and a healthy heart. I particularly worry about the effect on children of all the trans fats they eat in bought fast food, pastries and other snack foods. They need good sources of omega-3 oils to compensate and ensure healthy growth and brain development.

Trans fats, like saturated fats, can also raise cholesterol levels – avoid them!

CREATING A BALANCED DIET

It's easy: follow the government's Balance of Health recommendations, which work perfectly for vegetarians and vegans. A portion is an average serving size, such as one slice of bread, an apple, or two tablespoons of cooked beans or vegetables. Every day, aim to eat:

5 portions of fruit and vegetables

Or more if you can manage them – the more the better! Have juice and/or fresh or dried fruit with your breakfast and as a snack, and at least one portion of fruit, vegetables or salad with every meal (potatoes and pulses don't count) and two with your main meal. Include green vegetables daily for optimum health.

5 portions of starchy foods

These include bread, pasta, rice, potatoes, sweetcorn, any of the whole grains such as buckwheat and quinoa, as well as dried beans and lentils, which are included here because they contain both protein and carbohydrate. For losing weight and keeping it off, there is evidence that eating pulses in place of grains may be very helpful: see page 16.

2–3 portions of high-protein foods

Pulses again, see above; also eggs, cheese, tofu, tempeh, Quorn, wheat protein, soya proteins, nuts and seeds.

2–3 portions of milk and dairy food

Milk and milk products or milk or yogurt made from soya (or rice or oats); make sure it is fortified with calcium.

0–3 portions of fatty and sugary food

Eat sparingly, the fewer the better, except for small quantities of the healthy fats: see Essential Fats, *facing page*.

GET SLIM AND STAY SLIM DO YOU WANT TO REACH YOUR IDEAL WEIGHT AND STAY THERE WITHOUT CONSTANT DIETING; TO FEEL HEALTHY AND FULL OF ENERGY EVERY DAY WITHOUT BLOATING, HEADACHES, ASSORTED ACHES AND PAINS; TO LOOK AND FEEL YOUNGER AND FITTER FOR LONGER?

Imagine what it would be like for the weight to steadily drop off you while you feel inwardly at peace, with no cravings for foods or drinks you can't have. Imagine what it would be like to have the confidence that comes from knowing you're looking your best, your eating is under control and you'll never again have to go on a diet.

The low-GI vegetarian (and vegan) diet will enable you to do just that. It's the nearest thing to a miracle that I've come across, a really effective way of getting to your perfect weight and staying there. The reason it works so well is that by sticking to low-GI foods (and in particular including plenty of beans and pulses in your meals), you keep your blood sugar at an even level and avoid the confusion of energy 'highs' and 'lows'. You never need to go hungry, because there's always something good you can eat.

If you consistently eat in the way described you will find that within about a fortnight, food cravings will simply melt away. You will feel so calm and centred you might even forget to eat – and then not feel you have to eat everything in sight, but eat normally. Your appetite will shrink naturally, the weight will drop off, and, because this is a way of eating based on normal foods and normal meals, it will stay off. As the weight drops off, you will naturally feel like exercising more, which will in turn speed up the weight-loss process.

You don't need will power because after a couple of weeks you'll find the foods you used to crave don't tempt you any more. But for best and quickest results, you need to be determined and focused. So stick to the simple principles of the diet and experience for yourself the remarkable results.

How much weight will you lose?
Most people lose an average of about 2 pounds/1 kilo a week, although some lose much more, especially early in the diet, and especially if they were carrying a lot of extra weight. One or two pounds (0.5 to 1 kilo) a week soon add up, especially as this diet very soon stops feeling like 'a diet' and becomes a way of eating you feel you could stay on for ever. But please don't keep weighing yourself! I'm convinced this is counterproductive. Give yourself a break from the tyranny of the bathroom scales. Weigh yourself on the day you start, then put the scales away and don't weigh yourself again until your clothes feel really loose.

Some people feel a little out of sorts and prone to headaches in the first week or so. This is the body readjusting, is quite natural and soon passes. Trust the low-GI way of eating, which has now been tried and tested by many thousands of people, trust your body, and just be happy and at peace as the pounds drop off – and continue to drop off. This happens so naturally that some people find they go on losing weight even after they reach the 'goal' they decided on, and

become skinnier than they dreamed possible –
but healthily so. The body knows when it's time
to stop, and does so naturally.

What you can eat

- Carbohydrates: you can eat unlimited
  quantities of fruit, vegetables and pulses;
  consume asterisked foods in the table
  sparingly – keep to the portion sizes on
  page 11 while losing weight.
- Proteins: pulses, also eggs, cheese (dairy and
  soya), tofu, unsweetened soya yogurt (Sojasun,
  from good health-food shops), tempeh,
  Quorn, soya proteins, soya nuts.
- Fats and oils: use a light non-hydrogenated
  margarine for spreading, and olive oil for
  cooking and salad dressings; small quantities of
  mayonnaise, especially light, are fine; eat small
  amounts of avocado – a quarter occasionally.
- Drinks and beverages: water, plain or sparkling;
  apple juice, freshly squeezed orange juice,
  skimmed milk, unsweetened soya milk, tea,
  herb tea and decaffeinated coffee – caffeine is
  best avoided as it increases insulin production
  in the body, which in turn reduces blood sugar
  and gives you feelings of 'false hunger'. Keep
  off alcohol while you're losing weight.
- Flavourings and seasonings: garlic, herbs and
  spices can be used freely, as can mustard,
  lemon and lime juice, vinegar, horseradish and
  tamari or soy sauce (unsweetened).
- Sugar and sweetenings: avoid sugar. Use small
  amounts of apple juice concentrate or raw
  organic honey, or a sweetener such as
  Splenda, or better still the herbal alternative
  Stevia (see page 164). Very tiny amounts of
  sugar in some bought sauces and seasonings
  don't matter (listed at the end of the

ingredients), but avoid anything that contains
more than a tiny amount, whether by its own
or any other name, such as corn syrup, corn
sugar, cane juice, cane sugar, beet sugar, barley
malt, caramel, carob syrup, maltodextrin,
sorbitol and any of the –oses: sucrose, glucose,
lactose, maltose, dextrose. Get sweetness
from actual fruits or fruit juices (without
added sugar) while you're losing weight.

Go easy on ...

- Wholegrain breads, cereals, grains. Although
  some wholegrain breads, cereals and grains
  are technically low GI, because of the amount
  of starch they contain they have to be eaten in
  limited quantities (see the GI Food Table on
  pages 10/11). Since it's easy to overeat these
  foods, and since some people are sensitive to
  wheat, I advise you to be sparing with them.
  Instead, eat corn thins and popcorn and fill up
  on pulses, sweetcorn, vegetables and fruit, all
  of which will help you to lose weight.

- Nuts and seeds are low GI and undoubtedly nutritious but they are high in fat and very moreish – once you start eating them, it's not easy to stop. For this reason, it's better not to have them at all if you're losing weight. Soya nuts, which you can buy in health shops or make yourself (see page 96), make an excellent alternative crunchy snack or garnish and you can eat them in virtually unlimited amounts. You can also buy soya-nut butter, which is a better option than peanut butter.
- Fats and dairy: eggs are fine, but avoid butter and go very easy on the cheese. Having a little low-fat cottage cheese sometimes is fine, as is sprinkling some strongly flavoured cheese over foods for flavour, but keep it to the minimum. Soya-based vegan cheese, such as melting cheese slices, is fine.

MAKING IT WORK

This really is a simple diet. Just choose the foods listed under 'What you can eat' on page 17, eat them until you're full and satisfied – and watch the weight drop off. It really is that simple, but here are some tips to make it as easy and successful as possible.

Have a good breakfast

Starting the day without food inside you is like setting off on a car journey with an empty tank. There are lots of healthy low-GI foods you can eat to start the day. Here are some suggestions.

- Fresh fruit: my favourite. A fruit breakfast is surprisingly sustaining and a great way of getting several of your 'five a day'. You can splurge here and enjoy all the sweetest, juiciest fruits you like. Eat them as they are, make them into fruit salad or whiz them into a thick and luscious smoothie (you can add a banana for this, see page 120): quick, easy and delicious.
- You can vary a fruit breakfast by serving it with some plain low-fat yogurt (soya or dairy) or some low-fat cottage cheese, or by heating it: baked apples or bananas make great hot breakfasts, as does dried fruit compote, page 168, perhaps with some chopped fresh fruit added to it.
- If you want a cereal or grain breakfast, you can't beat porridge (see page 121.) Or make oats into a fruity muesli by adding chopped or grated apple or pear mixed with plain low-fat yogurt (soya or dairy) and raisins, and sweetening it to taste.
- For a cooked breakfast, there's omelette, maybe filled with mushrooms or tomatoes, with a sprinkling of strongly flavoured cheese or chopped herbs; or scrambled egg (or tofu)

served on a Portobello mushroom or just one slice of stone-ground wholemeal or other very high-fibre bread.

- You could have a piece of Onion, Tomato and Basil Crustless Quiche, page 52, perhaps saved from the night before; or Bean 'Potato' Cakes, page 41, with grilled tomatoes and mushrooms.

Make time for lunch

- Eating beans or lentils in some form at lunchtime prevents an energy slump in the middle of the afternoon, and also means you are not tired and ravenous when it's time to make an evening meal. A mug or bowl of a pulse soup, such as Green Pea Soup with Mint, page 32, White Bean Soup, page 32 or a lentil soup, bought or homemade, either before or with lunch does the trick. Make a big pot at the weekend and keep it in the fridge or freezer.
- A bean salad is great, too. Try the Bean Salade Niçoise, page 91, or Chick Pea and Tomato Salad, page 93, or simply mix cooked or canned beans or lentils – one type, or a mixture of two or more – with any ingredients you fancy: chopped tomato, grated carrot, red pepper, spring onion, chopped mint, parsley, chives, tarragon or coriander and splash of wine vinegar, olive oil and seasoning. There are so many different pulses and flavourings that this can be different every day.
- Try a salad with a leafy base. Line a plate or a lunchbox with your favourite leaves, such as lettuce or watercress, then top with all the ingredients you like: slices of tomato, cucumber, cooked sweetcorn, radishes, cooked green beans, chopped red pepper, chopped herbs, then add some protein – some canned or cooked beans, home-made marinated tofu chunks or a little strongly flavoured cheese or sliced hard-boiled egg. Remember to pack a fork too.

- Dips or pâtés such as Light and Creamy Hummus, page 88, or Mediterranean Bean Pâté, page 89, with chunky lettuce heart, raw vegetable crudités or some corn thins are also ideal for lunch.
- If you must have a sandwich, then make it an open one, with a slice of stone-ground wholemeal or other very high-fibre bread spread with mustard or low-fat mayonnaise and topped with lettuce, tomato, cucumber, onion, red pepper – whatever you fancy – and then some cottage cheese or hard-boiled egg, too, if you wish. Corn thins also make good sandwiches – filled with a bean burger, any of the bean dips, some soya-nut butter or sliced tomato and a very small amount of strongly flavoured cheese or a slice of vegan cheese – but make them at the last minute so they stay crisp.
- Leftovers from supper can make a welcome lunch if you have heating facilities. There are lots you could try: Pistou, page 87, Thai Beancakes, page 94, Best-ever Chilli, page 101, Slow-cook Black Beans, page 98. Or for one that doesn't need heating, mix Quick Grilled Mediterranean Vegetables, page 43, with drained chick peas and a sprinkling of crumbled feta cheese or some Marinated Tofu, page 145.

Evening meal ideas

It does make sense to eat more during the day when you're burning up the energy rather than stoking up in the evening before going to sleep. I used to find this difficult to do until I started eating the GI way, and, in particular, eating beans or lentils in some form for lunch. I began to find I wasn't so hungry in the evening: some fruit, a little salad, a few steamed vegetables with some homemade tomato sauce was enough.

So don't be surprised if after you've been doing the diet for a few weeks you find the same, and don't feel you have to eat a main meal in the evening if you don't have the appetite for one. However, if you are hungry, there are plenty of delicious possibilities.

- Chunky Oven Ratatouille, page 48, with Bean Mash, page 41.
- Spinach Curry, page 60, with Lentil Dal, page 109, and Tomato and Coriander Chutney, page 70, or Quick Tofu Curry with Peas, page 150.
- Golden Thai Curry, page 42, making the low-fat version, served with Grilled Spiced Tofu with Peppers, page 148, or Thai Beancakes, page 94.
- Any of the pasta recipes using 40g (1½ oz) dry weight pasta with a large salad, and have some protein, such as a little cheese, or yogurt for pudding.
- Pizza Bake, page 103, with a side salad or cooked green vegetable if you like.
- Onion, Tomato and Basil Crustless Quiche, page 52, with salad or seasonal vegetables such as green beans or spinach.
- Egg Fu Yong, page 53, or Asian Soya Beans, page 96.

Snacks

- Green Pea Soup with Mint, page 32.
- Lentil and Vegetable Soup, page 84.
- Leek, Chick Pea and Saffron Soup, page 85.
- Lentil and Cumin Cakes, page 92.
- Raw vegetable crudités.
- Corn thins.
- Popcorn, homemade, with a little olive oil and salt.
- Soya nuts, with or without raisins.
- Fruit – especially if you fancy something sweet.
- Edamame beans in their pods, see page 64.

Tips

- Tune into and respond to your appetite. Eat when you're hungry.
- Always eat until you're really full and satisfied.
- Eat plenty of bean or lentil soups for low-GI satisfaction and a feeling of being replete.
- Eat fruit before you go out for an evening meal.
- Avoid the tyranny of the bathroom scales – don't weigh yourself every day. You might not want to weigh yourself at all.
- When you can, eat lighter at night.

CURING CRAVINGS

By sticking to the 'unlimited' low-GI foods, you will break your addictions to sugar and refined carbohydrates. Soon, instead of craving bread, crisps, sweets, desserts, or whatever you used to want, you'll be amazed to find that you fancy sweet fruit and filling, comforting beans – and getting thinner and healthier by the minute. You may find this hard to believe right now, but it does happen. The trick is to work out what you fancy and to satisfy your craving with low-GI foods, which you can eat freely.

- If you crave desserts, chocolate or anything sweet, then you want a sugar hit, so eat all you like of the sweetest, juiciest fruits you can find. Keep a bowl of fruit salad, made with your favourite fruits, in your fridge for easy snacking, whiz up silky fruit smoothies or try hot sweet puddings like baked apples or bananas.

- If you crave potatoes or pasta, then you are after comforting 'stodge', so fill up on all the permissible starchy foods – lentils, beans, peas, sweetcorn – you can eat. Try lovely creamy Bean Mash, page 41, or 'Potato' Cakes, page 41, a soothing bowl of bean or lentil soup, canned (check the label) or homemade from easy recipes in this book (pages 84 and 85), or try Lentil and Cumin Cakes, page 92, which have a comforting consistency.

- If you crave bread – again, hit that comforting stodge spot with beans and sweetcorn, as described above. For a sandwich or bun replacement, try corn thins topped with a bean burger, bean dip, a little strong cheese or soya cheese slices, which can be melted under the grill for a cheese-on-toast effect. For peanut butter cravings, try spreading corn thins with soya-nut butter.

- If you crave crisps or nuts, it may be salt, 'crunch' or protein you're after. Satisfy them all with a handful of soya nuts, either on their own or mixed with raisins, or try some homemade salty popcorn – as much as you can eat, tossed with a little olive oil or olive oil spray. Crunchy corn thins are also good.

MAKE SURE YOU EAT ENOUGH

When you first start doing the diet, it's important that you eat enough. Fill up on the low-GI 'unlimited' foods until you're totally full and satisfied. Give yourself permission to eat as much as you want of these foods. You may not lose weight during this initial period, but this feeling of freedom will relax you, stabilize your blood sugar and change your taste buds.

Very soon – usually within 7 to 14 days, certainly within a month – you'll realize you're feeling much calmer and steadier in energy, and, even more remarkably, that the food cravings have gone. You will also realize, perhaps to your surprise, that you are not thinking about food all the time, you don't feeling very hungry and you are naturally eating less. Sometimes you'll even be surprised that you have to remind yourself it's time for a meal.

This is part of the magic of this diet. It is extraordinary how the cravings cease and how your appetite shrinks; and, of course, the more it shrinks, the less you want to eat and the more weight you lose, and so it goes on. It's a remarkably natural, healthy process. In time, your body finds its natural weight and stays there. But in order to achieve this, you must eat plenty at first. I can't emphasize this enough! Eat all you want of the recommended low-GI foods, trust your body, trust the diet and you'll be amazed and thrilled at the results.

EATING FOR TWO VEGETARIANS AND VEGANS REALLY CAN PRODUCE PERFECT, HEALTHY CHILDREN. BABIES ARE BEING BORN TO FOURTH- AND FIFTH-GENERATION VEGETARIANS AND VEGANS IN THE UK NOW, AND OF COURSE AROUND THE WORLD WHOLE CULTURES HAVE BEEN VEGETARIAN FOR THOUSANDS OF YEARS.

If you're planning to have a baby in the near future, you can give it the best possible start by preparing in advance. As some forms of the contraceptive pill may reduce the absorption of nutrients, it's a good idea to check with your doctor or use another form of contraception while you prepare for pregnancy; you would also be wise to cut back on alcohol and caffeine.

Build up your health and vitality with a good diet, as described on pages 8–15. In particular, make sure your intake of vitamins B12 and D is adequate (see page 13), and that you're getting enough of the other B vitamins, especially folic acid, as well as iron and vitamin E, by eating plenty of dark-green leafy vegetables (at least one good serving every day), yeast extract, pulses and wholegrain cereals, and have a good portion of protein at every meal. Include some omega-3 oils every day, such as flaxseeds or oil, cold-pressed rapeseed oil, walnuts and walnut oil, and consider taking a vegetarian omega-3 supplement (see page 192) or including omega-3 enriched eggs in your diet. Eat lots of fruit (especially oranges and orange juice for folic acid) and vegetables, and drink plenty of water.

Because it's such an important vitamin for pregnancy, health experts advise that, in addition to a healthy diet, it's important to take a 400 mcg supplement of folic acid while you're preparing for pregnancy and until you're twelve weeks pregnant.

If you've been eating as described, you'll be off to a really good start and can continue in the same way once you're pregnant. Even if you haven't been able to prepare, it's never too late, and pregnancy is a brilliant time to improve your diet, and to nurture yourself and the new life growing inside you. You'll need slightly increased amounts of vitamins A, B1, B2, C, D and folic acid than usual throughout your pregnancy, but your requirement for minerals such as iron, calcium, magnesium, zinc and iodine doesn't change, because your body is working more efficiently and absorbing more nutrients. If you think you may not be getting all the nutrients you need, it might be wise to take a vitamin supplement. Choose one that has been specially formulated for pregnancy, without too much vitamin A, which has been associated with birth defects: check with your ante-natal clinic or pharmacist if in doubt.

You don't need to eat an awful lot more when you're pregnant, just an extra 200 calories during the last three months, easily supplied by a nutritious snack such as those described opposite. It's when the baby has arrived and you're breastfeeding that you really have to 'eat for two', because then you need 500 extra calories. If you don't eat enough, you may not produce as much milk. You also need to make sure you drink plenty of water. At first it's hard even to find time to make meals for yourself, so having several good-quality snacks instead could be more practical.

Healthy snacks

- Light and Creamy Hummus (page 88) with crudités or bread.
- Wholemeal watercress sandwiches with yeast extract.
- A bowl of Lentil and Vegetable Soup (page 84).
- A handful of nuts and seeds with dried fruit.
- A piece of Sticky Parkin (page 182).
- An almond or banana smoothie (page 120), perhaps with an extra spoonful of molasses.
- Soya or dairy yogurt with a chopped banana and a sprinkling of chopped almonds or wheat germ.
- A bowl of Muesli or Granola, or Iron-rich Breakfast Mix (page 120), with milk or soya milk.
- Wholegrain nut butter sandwiches, perhaps with some yeast extract and salad.
- Lentil Dal (page 109) with brown basmati rice.
- A bowl of creamy porridge (made with half water, half milk), topped with flaked almonds, chopped almonds or ground hazelnuts.
- Brown rice with cooked spinach and onion.
- A bowl of Dried Fruit Compote (page 168) with molasses and pistachios.

What to avoid

The Department of Health advises that pregnant women avoid the following foods during pregnancy because of the risk of salmonella or listeria:

- All unpasteurized milk (cow, sheep or goat).
- Soft-whip ice cream.
- Raw egg (watch out in desserts or home-made mayonnaise).
- Vegetable pâté (unless cooked or pasteurized).
- Ripened soft cheeses such as Camembert, Brie and some blue-veined varieties; also Gruyère.
- Some ready-made salads, such as potato.

In addition, prepared salads need to be washed again thoroughly before eating, while cook-chill meals must be thoroughly heated until piping hot.

Iron-boosting ideas

If you need to increase your iron level, here are some ideas. A week or so of concentrated 'iron snacking' can really help.

- Choose an iron-rich grain such as millet or wholewheat pasta in preference to rice; almonds, preferably blanched (because the skins can hinder iron absorption); and pumpkin seeds. Try eating the Iron-rich Breakfast Mix (page 120). This can supply up to 25 mg iron.
- Concentrate on the pulses that are highest in iron – lentils and soya beans. Eat soya nuts. Add a little soya flour to your cooking where possible, in sauces and casseroles, and sprinkle nutritional yeast flakes over your food.
- Eat plenty of dark-green leafy vegetables: 450 g (1 lb) spinach or kale, sautéed with an onion and garlic in oil, then served on brown rice, is an iron-rich meal, or you could prepare 1 kg (2¼ lb) organic carrots juiced with 225 g (8 oz) parsley, stalks and all – it's quite strong, so you might like to juice it in two or three batches.
- Snack on dried fruit, and try the iron-rich variation of the Dried Fruit Compote (see page 168): eaten in small servings over a day, this can provide up to 20 mg of iron. You can also drink prune juice, which is much more palatable than it sounds (especially with a shot of soda water), or use it to moisten your breakfast cereal (it's good with muesli).
- Take some blackstrap molasses daily. Try it straight from the spoon, or dissolved in milk or mixed with a little honey, or in compotes or parkin.

NURTURING THE NEXT GENERATION RESEARCH HAS SHOWN THAT A WELL-BALANCED VEGETARIAN DIET IS HEALTHY FOR BOTH CHILDREN AND BABIES AND PROVIDES ALL THE NOURISHMENT NEEDED. THIS IS NOW WIDELY ACKNOWLEDGED AMONG HEALTH PROFESSIONALS, INCLUDING ORGANIZATIONS SUCH AS THE BRITISH DIETETIC ASSOCIATION.

BABIES

As well as being a healthy choice, it's quite safe to bring a child up as a vegetarian or vegan. Indeed I have myself brought up three healthy daughters on a vegetarian diet. The important thing is to make sure you include plenty of nutrient-rich foods in their diet. Where concern has been expressed over the growth of babies and children on vegetarian-type diets, they were in communities following very restrictive rather than typical vegetarian or vegan diets.

There's no doubt that breastfeeding your baby, even if it's only for a few weeks, will give him or her the best possible start. However, if you don't want to, or can't breastfeed your baby, there are formula milks which are fine for vegetarians. If you're vegan, you may wonder about the advisability of using soya baby milks, since some concern has been expressed regarding their safety. However, of all those babies who have been raised on soya milk over the last twenty years, studies on humans have not demonstrated any adverse effects overall (apart from allergic reactions in susceptible infants) and there have been literally hundreds of studies demonstrating the positive effects of soya generally.

Weaning

Weaning is the process of gradually introducing solid food into a milk diet until a baby is eating normal meals. You can start the weaning process by offering some little tastes of solid food once your baby is four months old. Over the weeks, gradually increase the amount of solid food so that the baby is taking less and less milk; by about eight months most babies will eat some solids three times a day before their milk feeds, which remain very important both nutritionally and emotionally. Eventually they will drop the milk feeds one by one, so that by the time they're a year old they will be eating three meals a day, though many babies will continue with their night-time feed or bottle for at least another year.

Start with half a teaspoon of your chosen food, either before or after a milk feed, at lunchtime or in the evening, whichever is the most convenient. Good foods with which to start the weaning process are mashed ripe banana, peach, pear or avocado; puréed cooked apple, carrot or sweet potato; or a thin porridge made from baby rice (choose a plain, unsweetened one), flaked millet or quinoa.

As your baby takes more solid food and less milk, you will need to add other nutritious ingredients to the basic fruit and vegetable purées. Puréed lentils (made from split red lentils, without spices or seasoning but with a little walnut, flaxseed or rapeseed oil for extra energy and omega-3 oils) are brilliant; so are mashed tofu, live soya yogurt, very finely ground nuts and seeds (ground almonds are handy), tahini or home-made unsalted hummus, organic nut butters, nutritional yeast (from health food shops), beans (including baked beans without added salt, sugar or sweeteners), and some low-salt yeast extract fortified with vitamin B12. If you're bringing your baby up as a vegan, do make sure you include vitamin B12-fortified foods and ask your doctor about a vitamin D supplement.

Babies need small, frequent meals of concentrated nutrients; avoid too many watery or bulky foods and be sure to include the concentrated sources of energy and protein described above. Also include iron-rich foods daily, like soaked and puréed dried apricots, fortified cereals, molasses, red lentils, beans and dark green vegetables. Give these foods alongside fruit and vegetable juices, which are good sources of vitamin C, for maximum iron absorption.

Baby food notes and tips

- For the first six months, don't give wheat, nuts, seeds, eggs, citrus fruits or cows' milk, and no dairy foods at all if there is a history of allergies in your family. Ask your health visitor for advice.

- Mix nutritious but strong-tasting vegetables, including broccoli and kale, with a sweet vegetable such as sweet potato, squash or parsnip. They'll go down a treat that way.

- Cook tiny pasta shapes and mash with vegetables and a protein ingredient for a balanced meal.

- Go on increasing the variety of foods, mashing or sieving family foods for your baby to share, as long as they don't contain added salt (which can put a strain on the baby's kidneys), or too much spice or any other banned foods.

- If there is a history of allergies in your family, avoid nuts for the first three years, and don't give whole nuts to any child under five.

- Avoid foods containing sugar, including rusks and sweet biscuits.

- The manufacturers of Quorn recommend that it is not given to children under two years, and the same applies to other textured vegetable proteins. It's my view that cooked beans, lentils, grains, tofu, tempeh and seitan are preferable to these at any age.

- Continue breastfeeding or with infant formula as the main milk drink until one year. Full fat cows' milk can then be introduced. Don't give semi-skimmed milk to children under two years, and don't give skimmed milk to children under five. If you're using soya milk instead of cows' milk, it's best to choose one that has been fortified with calcium and vitamins B12 and D, or make up and use a soya formula baby milk.

CHILDREN AND TEENAGERS

The foods described for weaning your baby – pulses, whole grains and vegetables, enriched with protein, and in some cases ingredients high in fat – continue to offer the best nourishment for a growing child. Many of the recipes in this book are suitable for, and popular with, children. I am all for having shared meals, enjoyed by children and adults alike, as often as possible. Favourite family main courses include Best-ever Chilli (page 101), served with cooked rice or baked potatoes (if you use rice, any left-over chilli and rice can be mashed together, formed into burger shapes, rolled in dried crumbs and fried to make a meal for the children another day); Lentil and Cumin Cakes (page 92); Spaghetti with Red Hot Sauce (page 67); and Pizza Bake (page 103).

It's far better for your children if you limit shop-bought biscuits and cakes, sweetened and fizzy drinks, and salty snacks such as crisps. It helps to be prepared, with plenty of good foods available for snacks (see opposite). However, try not to get too tense about the situation; remember, a child who has a basically healthy diet, as described in this book, can withstand a little 'junk' food now and then.

OLDER CHILDREN

As children get older, especially if they're lively and love sports, their need for high-energy foods will increase. The answer, strange as it may seem, is the same as that described for healthy weaning and toddler food (both are periods of fast growth and high energy output): to keep to the healthy balance of carbohydrate, protein and fruit or vegetables, as shown opposite, boosted with foods which are energy- and nutrient-rich.

Nuts and seeds are excellent for this. They can be eaten whole, roasted, tossed in soy sauce then crisped under the grill or in the oven, or ground and sprinkled over breakfast cereals and mueslis, salads, cooked grains and vegetables, stir-frys and pasta dishes, stirred into shakes, or eaten as snacks. Tahini, peanut butter, or the more unusual and delectable almond, walnut or hazelnut butters you can get at health food shops, can be spread on bread, toast, oatcakes and crispbreads, or drizzled over chopped banana or Dried Fruit Compote (page 168). Light and Creamy Hummus (page 88), rich with tahini, is a wonderfully healthy spread and dip for snacking, and is also great over baked potatoes.

Dried fruit is good for concentrated sugar, some B vitamins, iron and calcium. It can be added to mueslis and cereals, flapjacks (see page 179) or fruit breads, soaked and made into puddings, and of course makes a handy snack on its own, perhaps with nuts and seeds.

It's also useful to have a supply of canned or cooked beans and cooked brown rice for instant healthy snacking. Heated up – or eaten cold as a salad – and served with some chopped avocado or a swirl of olive oil (or cold-pressed flaxseed or rapeseed oil for their omega-3 content), they're very filling and nutritious. If getting enough calories is a problem, these good-quality oils can be drizzled over almost anything.

Tofu, tempeh and seitan are particularly good for this age group, too, because of their high protein content. They can be simply fried and served on wholemeal bread, packed into burger buns or pitta bread, or eaten with Tahini or Peanut Sauce (page 147) for even more protein and nourishment.

Healthy snacks for children

- A healthy dip such as Light and Creamy Hummus (see page 88), guacamole, or one of the other dips on pages 88–89, with ready-prepared crudités, or rye or wheat bread fingers for dipping.
- Fresh fruit.
- A handful of raisins or other dried fruit.
- Nuts or soya nuts for children over five years.
- Cubes of cheese or marinated tofu.
- Oatcakes or corn thins, toast or sandwiches, with nut butters, tahini, miso, yeast extract, tofu spread or all-fruit jam or apricot purée (page 168).
- A handful of drained, cooked chick peas or red kidney beans.
- Tempeh Burgers (page 151).
- Little Provençal Pancakes (page 106) with tomato ketchup (choose a healthy one), or honey, or all-fruit jam.
- A slice of Sticky Date Bread (page 183) or Sticky Parkin (page 182).
- A bowl of cereal with cow's or soya milk.
- A smoothie (page 120).
- Baked potato with a spoonful of Light and Creamy Hummus (page 88) or some grated cheese.
- Water, or real fruit juice diluted with water.

Daily servings for children (1–5 years)

This is just a guide – every child is different, and the servings can be adapted according to the age and needs of the individual child.

- Grains and cereals: 4–5 servings, including wholegrain bread, rice, pasta, unsweetened wholegrain breakfast cereals and potatoes.
- Pulses, nuts, seeds: 1–2 servings, including nut butters, tahini, lentils and mashed beans.
- Dairy or soya: 3 servings, including milk, cheese, hard-boiled free-range eggs, yogurt, fortified soya milk and tofu.
- Vegetables: 2–3 servings, preferably including green leafy vegetables.
- Fruit: 1–3 servings, with dried fruit at least once every few days.

ORGANICS FOR CHILDREN The effect of chemical residues from artificial fertilizers, pesticides and other sprays used on non-organic food is greater on children because of their smaller body weight and immature, developing systems. We do not know what long-term damage these, or genetically modified ingredients, may do, but I think it's worth paying a bit extra for organic produce for peace of mind. By doing so, you also avoid hydrogenated fats and, by supporting organic producers, help to promote forms of production which benefit the environment.

LOOK YOUNGER, LIVE LONGER IF YOU WANT TO FIND THE KEY TO LOOKING YOUNGER AND LIVING LONGER, YOU CAN DO NO BETTER THAN STUDY THE LIFESTYLE OF THE PEOPLE OF THE JAPANESE ISLANDS OF OKINAWA, WHERE THERE ARE MORE CENTENARIANS THAN ANYWHERE ELSE IN THE WORLD, WHERE THE PEOPLE STAY HAPPY AND ACTIVE THROUGHOUT THEIR LIVES — AND WHERE THEY EAT A LOW-GI DIET!

Okinawa is an archipelago of 161 islands stretching for 1300km (800 miles) between the Japanese main islands and Taiwan, and the home of the longest-lived people in the world, people who seem to have beaten the ageing process, for whom heart disease is minimal, breast cancer so rare that screening is unnecessary, and where most men have never heard of prostate cancer. In fact in Okinawa the three leading killers in the West — heart disease, stroke and cancer — occur with the lowest frequency in the world, and dementia rates among the elderly are markedly lower than in America and Japan. To quote from *The Okinawa Way* by Bradley Willcox (MD), Craig Willcox (PhD) and Makoto Suzuki (MD), which describes what doctors learned from a twenty-five-year study of these people, the centenarians of Okinawa 'have slim, lithe bodies, sharp clear eyes, quick wits, passionate interests, and the kind of Shangri-la glow that we all covet'.

So what is their secret? As you might expect, there are a number of lifestyle factors including their Eastern tradition and wisdom, spiritual beliefs, supportive community, regular exercise and diet, which undoubtedly contribute to the health and longevity of the Okinawans. Here, I'm going to concentrate on their diet and what it can show us about eating for health and longevity.

One of the most striking things about the Okinawan diet is the amount of complex carbohydrates — whole grains and grain products — and fresh vegetables of all kinds that it contains: a staggering 7–13 servings of each group every day! In addition to this, they eat 2–4 servings of fruit, 2–4 servings of pulses and soya products, especially tofu, small quantities of seaweed, small amounts of oil and a wide variety of herbs and spices each day. They eat minimal amounts of dairy produce, which, combined with seaweed, makes up just 2 per cent of their diet. They also eat 1–3 servings of fish and other omega-3 foods every day, and occasionally pork. Their total intake of fats is only 24 per cent, compared with around 40 per cent in America and the UK, and their main cooking oil is cold-pressed rapeseed oil.

Apart from the fish and occasional pork, this diet plan is remarkably similar to that of a low-GI vegetarian — and, in particular, vegan — diet. This may explain why vegetarians and vegans share the same low rates for heart disease and some cancers as the Okinawans. So, you're off to an excellent start if you follow these guidelines:

- Eat plenty of fruit and vegetables. You don't have to chew your way through massive salads. Make quick, easy-to-eat soups and casseroles, or invest in an inexpensive juicer.
- Include soya products, such as calcium-fortified tofu, soya milk and yogurt, miso, soya sprouts, soya nuts and green soya beans (see picture) every day.

- Base your meals on whole grains and pulses. Of the grains, well-cooked quinoa and buckwheat are particularly digestible. Buckwheat is especially good because of its effect on the circulation.
- Use cold-pressed rapeseed or olive oil for cooking, but only over a gentle heat.
- Include daily sources of the omega-3 oils (powdered flaxseeds, flaxseed oil, walnuts and walnut oil), which the Okinawans get from the fish they eat, as well as from flaxseeds and (small amounts) from tofu. Consider taking an algae-based omega-3 vitamin supplement (page 14) or eating omega-3 enriched eggs for an extra boost.
- Limit your consumption of alcohol (Okinawan women might have one small drink a day, the men, two), but drink plenty of water, green tea and jasmine tea.
- Eat as wide a variety of foods, mainly from plant sources, as you can. The Okinawans were found to eat 206 foods over the course of a year, eating 38 different foods regularly and an average of 18 different foods a day.
- Don't eat too much salt.
- Be sure to get enough vitamin D – sit outside in the summer, even if you only uncover your hands, face and neck. Take a supplement (no more than 10 mcg daily) if in any doubt.

Natural menopause

Women in Okinawa experience the menopause naturally, without any drugs and with fewer complications such as hot flushes or hip fractures. They get natural oestrogens from their diet, mainly from the large quantities of soya they consume. Soya contains phyto-oestrogens, or plant oestrogens, called flavonoids. Other major

phyto-oestrogens are lignans, which come from flax and other grains. In fact, all plants, especially pulses, onions and broccoli, contain these natural oestrogens, although not nearly in the same quantities as soya and flax. The good thing about flavonoids and lignans is that they help to protect you from any damaging effects of oestrogen while allowing you all the beneficial effects.

Foods for longevity

- Turmeric, which has been shown to have numerous healing powers (see page 60).
- Sweet potatoes, which are rich in vitamin A, are sweet and filling, yet won't make your blood sugar rise (unlike ordinary potatoes).
- Kuzu or arrowroot (see page 159).
- Seaweed – kombu, nori, hijiki, wakame (see page 124).
- Blueberries.
- Squash, carrots, courgettes, peppers, onions.
- Sprouted beans (see page 71).

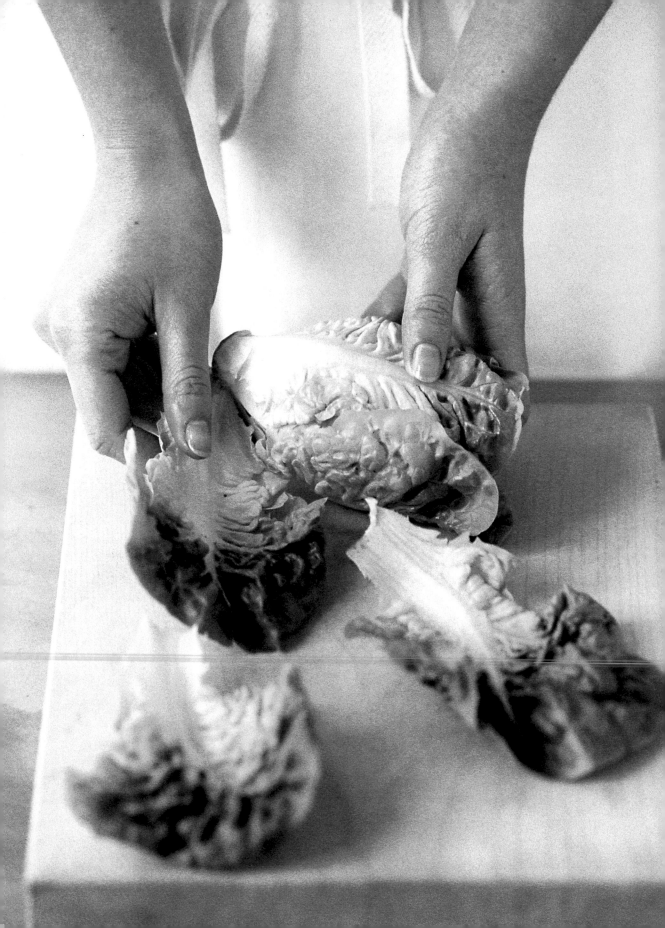

SALADS AND VEGETABLES

ONE OF THE REASONS WHY A LOW-GI VEGETARIAN OR VEGAN DIET IS SO HEALTH-GIVING IS BECAUSE OF ALL THE FRESH VEGETABLES IT CONTAINS: RAW, COOKED, IN STARTERS AND MAIN COURSES, AS ACCOMPANIMENTS … MANY MEALS CONSIST OF 'VEG AND TWO VEG', AND THEY'RE SO VARIED, COLOURFUL AND DELICIOUS THAT IT'S NO PROBLEM AT ALL TO EAT THE RECOMMENDED FIVE PORTIONS A DAY – IN FACT MANY VEGETARIANS EAT AT LEAST DOUBLE THAT. ORGANIC VEGETABLES ARE BEST IF YOU CAN GET THEM, BUT DON'T BE PUT OFF IF YOU CAN'T; ANY VEGETABLES ARE GREAT.

GREEN PEA SOUP WITH MINT ★

This is so easy and so good. The simple method is unusual but really effective, and the finishing touch is a swirl of thick yogurt and some fresh mint leaves. It's also lovely served chilled.

serves 4

900 g (2 lb) packet of frozen petit pois,
 or podded fresh peas if available
I large onion, roughly chopped
6 garlic cloves

TO FINISH
3–4 tablespoons thick plain yogurt
fresh mint leaves

Put the peas into a saucepan with 1.2 litres (2 pints) water, the onion and garlic. Cover and simmer for 10–15 minutes, until the onion and garlic are tender.

Whiz in a food processor until puréed, then return to the saucepan. Thin, if necessary, with a little more water and season with salt and freshly ground black pepper. Reheat, then ladle into bowls, top with a swirl of yogurt, a grinding of black pepper and mint leaves, and serve.

WHITE BEAN SOUP Use four 410g cans of butter beans (without added sugar) or other white beans, drained and rinsed, instead of the peas. Chop the onion and fry in 1 tablespoon of olive oil in a covered pan for 10 minutes until tender, then purée with the beans and enough water or vegetable stock to make a creamy consistency. Simmer in a pan for about 10 minutes. Add salt and pepper and chopped parsley. Lightly fried chopped mushrooms make a pleasant addition.

TOMATO AND RED PEPPER SOUP WITH AVOCADO ★

Tomato soup appeals to all age groups, and this one is particularly
delicious, with the added sweetness of red peppers.

serves 6

4 red peppers
750 g (1 lb 10 oz) tomatoes
1 onion, roughly chopped
2 fat garlic cloves
600 ml (1 pint) vegetable stock
juice of ½ a lemon
1 medium avocado
6 tablespoons dairy or soya cream
6 basil leaves, torn

Halve, seed and roughly chop the peppers, then quarter the tomatoes. Put them into a saucepan with the onion, garlic cloves and stock.

Simmer for 30 minutes until the peppers are very tender. Purée in a blender or food processor, then pass through a sieve into a clean saucepan. Reheat, and season with salt, pepper and some of the lemon juice.

Peel, stone and finely dice the avocado. Place in a bowl, toss in the remaining lemon juice and season with salt.

Ladle the soup into warmed bowls. Swirl each bowl with a little cream, then top with a spoonful of avocado, some torn basil leaves and a scattering of coarsely ground black pepper.

BRAISED VEGETABLES WITH LEMON AND PARSLEY ★

This is a very useful, not to mention delicious dish, which can be made in advance and re-heated – it just goes on getting better. It's also good cold if there's any left over. It's lovely served with some Bean Mash, page 41.

serves 4

pared zest and juice of 1 lemon
4 tablespoons olive oil
bunch of flat-leaf parsley
2 bay leaves
2 or 3 sprigs of thyme
4 large carrots, cut into batons
2 red peppers, seeded and cut into chunks
225 g (8 oz) broccoli, cut into florets
225 g (8 oz) mangetout, halved lengthwise
bunch of salad onions, trimmed

Put the pared lemon zest into a large saucepan with the olive oil, 125 ml (4 fl oz) water, the stalks of the parsley, the bay leaves and sprigs of thyme.

Bring to the boil, then add the carrots. Simmer for about 5 minutes, to par-cook the carrots, then add the peppers and cook for a further 5 minutes.

Add the broccoli and cook for about 4 minutes, until it is beginning to soften, then add the mangetout and salad onions and cook for a further 2 minutes or so, until they're just tender.

Pour in the lemon juice and season with salt and pepper. Just before serving, remove the bay leaves, chop the remaining parsley and stir in.

LITTLE GEM, CHICORY AND WATERCRESS SALAD ★

This is a fresh-tasting mixture of contrasting leaves with a thick golden mustard dressing. You can vary the leaves – a packet of mixed baby leaves is nice if you want a change from watercress.

serves 2–4

2 Little Gem lettuces
2 heads of chicory
bunch or packet of watercress

FOR THE MUSTARD VINAIGRETTE
1 teaspoon Dijon mustard
½ a garlic clove, crushed
1 tablespoon red wine vinegar
    or cider vinegar
3 tablespoons olive oil

Cut the lettuces into thick wedges – sixths or eighths – right down through their stems. Remove the outer leaves from the chicory, then cut the hearts into quarters or eighths. If you're using bunched watercress, which is great if you can get it, remove the thickest part of the stems. Wash all the leaves and shake dry, then heap them up on a serving dish or put them into a salad bowl.

For the vinaigrette, put the mustard, garlic, vinegar and a little salt into a bowl and mix with a fork or small whisk, then gradually whisk in the oil. Season to taste.

To serve, drizzle the vinaigrette over and around the salad, and grind some black pepper coarsely over.

VINAIGRETTE FOR A PARTY Generally I mix up a dressing as and when I need it, often straight into the salad bowl. However, there are times when it's handy to make up a batch for a party, or to keep a bottle in the fridge. To make about 200 ml (7 fl oz), increase the quantities given to 1 tablespoon of Dijon mustard, 1 large garlic clove, 3 tablespoons of red wine vinegar or cider vinegar and 9 tablespoons of olive oil, with some salt and pepper to taste. Simply shake together in a jar or bottle until emulsified. This will keep well in the fridge for several weeks; just give it a shake before you use it.

MARINATED OLIVES ★

Wonderful as a nibble, simple salad accompaniment or quick starter –
just serve with some good bread – and so pretty. Buy the best unstoned
olives you can find – I like a mixture of Kalamata and green Queen olives.

serves 4

**250 g (9 oz) mixed (unstoned) olives,
  including Kalamata and green Queen olives**
pared zest of 1 organic orange
1 large garlic clove, thinly sliced
¼ teaspoon dried red chilli flakes
½ teaspoon coriander seeds
½ teaspoon fennel seeds
1–2 tablespoons chopped flat-leaf parsley
2 tablespoons freshly squeezed orange juice
2 tablespoons fruity olive oil

Put the olives into a bowl with all the other ingredients and mix together. Leave for at least 1 hour –
longer if possible – for the flavours to mingle.

QUICK WAYS WITH VEGETABLES

SPINACH

For spinach, you don't need any water. Just cram all the leaves into a large saucepan. They'll soon produce their own liquid and can bubble away for 4–8 minutes, or until tender. It helps to push them down into the pan and sort of chop them at the same time with the end of a fish slice. Drain well in a colander once they're tender.

WONDERFUL BRUSSELS SPROUTS

I know lots of people hate Brussels sprouts, and I do too unless they're done my mother's way! Choose tiny, hard ones, trim as necessary and then – and this is the important bit – cut them completely in half. Cook them in 1–2.5 cm (½–1 in) boiling water in a lidded pan for no longer than 5–6 minutes, until they're only just tender, then drain immediately, return to the pan with a good knob of butter or a swirl of oil, and salt, freshly ground black pepper and grated nutmeg or a dash of celery salt to taste, and tell me they're not wonderful.

PERFECT GREEN VEGETABLES

The secret of cooking vegetables such as cabbage, French beans and all leaves except spinach, is to use just a little water – 1–2.5 cm (½–1 in) in the bottom of the pan. Bring it to the boil, then add the vegetables – make sure the cabbage is well shredded – and put the lid on. This means they half boil, half steam, and most cook in anything from 4 to 8 minutes. Keep testing until they're just right for you, then drain, add some salt and pepper, a swirl of oil or butter if you like, and serve. There's goodness and flavour in the water, so if you know you're going to need vegetable stock, it's worth keeping.

BEAN 'POTATO' CAKES

These are excellent. Make some Bean 'Mash' as described below. Vary the mixture as you wish with chopped parsley, drained canned sweetcorn (without added sugar) or even chopped cooked cabbage for a beany bubble and squeak. Form into 'cakes': you will get about three from one can. They hold together best if you bake them. Place them on an oiled baking sheet, then turn them over so that the tops are coated with oil. Bake at 200°C/400°F/Gas Mark 6 – for about 25 minutes, turning them after about 15 minutes.

BEAN 'MASH'

Mashed potatoes have a high GI rating but this Bean 'Mash' can hit that mashed potato spot. Not only does it look and taste very like mashed potatoes, it's also good in its own right. Use any white bean – butter beans work particularly well – soaked and cooked as described on page 82 or canned (without added sugar). Drain well. Fry a chopped onion in 1 tablespoon of olive oil and purée with the beans in a food processor or with a stick blender, or simply mash. Add 1 tablespoon of soya milk or water for each can of beans, salt and pepper, and whiz or beat again until thick and creamy. Chopped parsley, crushed garlic or fried onion are tasty additions. Also the basis for very good and versatile Bean 'Potato' Cakes, above.

COOKING POTATOES IN THEIR SKINS

Although potatoes have a high GI rating, you can reduce it by cooking them in their skins. Baby new potatoes, slightly under-cooked, have the lowest GI rating of any potatoes, and you can lower it further by tossing them in lemon juice, olive oil, chopped chives and perhaps some sliced cherry tomatoes. Bake jacket potatoes in a hot oven – 230°C/450°F/Gas Mark 8 – for 1–1½ hours, until crisp and crunchy on the outside and soft within. Eat them with something fibrous such as baked beans, or scoop out most of the inside and just eat the crunchy skins with salad or a creamy dip. Bircher potatoes (named after the Swiss doctor who came up with the idea; he also invented muesli) are also cooked with skins on and are delicious. Halve potatoes, rub all over with olive oil, place cut-side down on a baking sheet and bake as described above for about 45 minutes. They are done when the flesh is tender and the cut surface is crisp and golden brown.

GOLDEN THAI CURRY ★

This is very easy to make and everyone loves it. You can get freeze-dried lime leaves in the spices section of large supermarkets. This is a good recipe for slimming if you use the low-fat version (see below).

serves 4

1 tablespoon olive oil
1 tablespoon Thai red curry paste
1 red pepper, seeded and cut into 1 cm ($\frac{1}{2}$ in) pieces
1 golden pepper, seeded and cut into 1 cm ($\frac{1}{2}$ in) pieces
4 fat salad onions, chopped
1 medium courgette, cut into 1 cm ($\frac{1}{2}$ in) chunks
115 g (4 oz) baby sweetcorn, halved
115 g (4 oz) mangetout or sugarsnap peas
140 g (5 oz) baby button mushrooms, washed
400 ml can organic coconut milk or soya milk (see below)
6 lime leaves
$\frac{1}{2}$ teaspoon turmeric
2 garlic cloves, crushed
4 tablespoons fresh coriander, chopped

Heat the olive oil in a large saucepan or wok, then add the curry paste, followed by all the vegetables. Stir-fry for a few seconds, then cover and leave to cook for about 5 minutes, until nearly tender.

Add the coconut or soya milk, lime leaves, turmeric, garlic and some salt and pepper to taste. Stir, then sprinkle with chopped coriander and serve with some fried or marinated tofu and maybe a little hot cooked basmati rice.

LOW-FAT ALTERNATIVES FOR COCONUT MILK Although coconut milk has some health benefits, it is too high in fat to be used often in the low-GI way of eating, particularly if weight loss is your aim – even the lower-fat versions are quite high in calories. However, I have successfully used skimmed milk or unsweetened soya milk instead. You can even add a little coconut essence (see page 192), about $\frac{1}{4}$ teaspoon to 300 ml ($\frac{1}{2}$ pint) soya milk, to give a coconut flavour, though I have found that when a recipe contains many spices you don't miss the taste of the coconut that much.

QUICK GRILLED MEDITERRANEAN VEGETABLES ★

This is probably the fast meal that I fall back on most. Get your vegetables under the grill, then cook a grain or pasta to go with them. While these are cooking, whiz up some Light and Creamy Hummus (page 88) or some Bean 'Mash' (page 41) and you've got a meal in moments. I like to use a mixture of lemon juice and olive oil for the vegetables (the peppers don't need any) to keep them light. For a picture of this dish, turn to page 2.

serves 2–4

1–2 courgettes, halved or quartered lengthwise and cut into 5 cm (2 in) lengths
1 red onion, peeled and cut into sixths
1 aubergine, cut into chunky pieces
1 tablespoon olive oil
1 tablespoon fresh lemon juice
1 red and 1 yellow pepper, halved and seeded, then cut into strips
12 black olives (optional)
several sprigs of basil (optional)

Heat the grill to high. Put the courgette, onion and aubergine chunks on to a tray that will fit under your grill, add the olive oil, lemon juice and a little salt and move the vegetables around so that all get coated. I use my hands for this. Then add the pepper pieces – these don't need oiling as they cook fine without.

Grill for about 20 minutes, or until the vegetables are tender and browned in places, turning them around after 10 minutes.

Stir in the black olives and tear over some fresh basil, if using. Serve with a grain or pasta and some hummus or dal. If there are any vegetables left over, which hardly ever happens, they're great cold, too.

VARIATIONS Of course, you can vary the vegetables; sometimes I use just red peppers or mix them with olives, which makes a nice starter. Courgettes or aubergines, on their own, are also good, with chopped fresh mint mixed in at the end.

MUSHROOM PÂTÉ EN CROUTE

A pâté or terrine of mushrooms and nuts wrapped in puff pastry has long been a favourite dish of mine. While puff pastry is not low GI – and this is not a dish for slimmers – the nuts, wholemeal breadcrumbs and lemon juice all help to keep the GI within reasonable bounds, and it's wonderful for a special meal. Serve it with Madeira Gravy (page 146) and Cranberry Sauce (page 147), or some bought horseradish sauce.

serves 8

2 large onions, chopped
2 tablespoons olive oil
2 garlic cloves, chopped
250 g (9 oz) chestnut mushrooms, sliced roughly
225 g (8 oz) cashews, powdered in a food processor or coffee grinder
225 g (8 oz) ground almonds
225 g (8 oz) wholemeal breadcrumbs (stone-ground or very high fibre)
2 tablespoons soy sauce
2 tablespoons lemon juice
2 teaspoons dried tarragon
1 teaspoon yeast extract
500 g (1 lb 2 oz) puff pastry
beaten egg or soya milk, for brushing

Preheat the oven to 200°C/400°F/Gas Mark 6.

In a large saucepan, fry the onions in the olive oil for 7 minutes, until tender, then add the garlic and mushrooms and cook for a further 5 minutes, or until the mushrooms are tender. Then tip the mixture into a food processor and blend to a purée.

Put the ground cashew nuts and almonds into a bowl with the breadcrumbs, the mushroom purée, soy sauce, lemon juice, tarragon and yeast extract and mix well. It will be quite stiff. Season well with salt and pepper.

Roll the puff pastry out on a lightly floured board to make a square about 38 cm (15 in) in size. Transfer the pastry to a baking sheet and heap the mushroom mixture in the centre, forming it into a loaf shape.

Make diagonal cuts in the pastry about 1 cm (½ in) apart on each side of the mushroom mixture, then fold these up over the mushroom pâté to make a kind of plait effect. Tuck in the ends neatly, trim off any extra bits and brush with beaten egg or soya milk.

Bake for 40 minutes, or until the pastry is puffed and golden brown.

CUMIN-ROASTED SWEET POTATOES

Sweet potatoes cook much more quickly than you'd think: you can do them under the grill or on a barbecue and they always turn out well. I love them, children love them. Be sure to buy the type with pinkish flesh.

serves 4

1 kg (2 lb 4 oz) sweet potatoes, scrubbed
2 garlic cloves
2 tablespoons ground cumin
2 tablespoons olive oil
2 tablespoons fresh lemon juice

Heat the grill to high. Cut the sweet potatoes into chunky pieces about the size of walnuts and put on to a baking tray that will fit under your grill.

Chop or grate the garlic, then mix with a large pinch of salt and pound to a paste with the tip of your knife. Mix this paste with the cumin, olive oil, lemon juice and a little pepper, then mix it with the sweet potatoes so that they all get coated – I use my hands for this.

Grill for about 10–15 minutes, moving the potatoes around after about 5 minutes so they brown evenly. They're done when you can easily get a knife point into one and they're tinged brown.

An easy variation is to coat the sweet potatoes with just the olive oil and lemon juice, then sprinkle with steak seasoning, which you can get at any supermarket, before grilling.

TUMBET ★

A friend of mine told me about this Spanish dish, which she ate in
Majorca. It's a wonderful feast of vegetables that you can quickly
assemble, then put into the oven and forget about while they cook.
Use sweet potatoes instead of ordinary potatoes if you wish for a
deliciously sweet mixture with a lower GI rating, or leave out the
potato element altogether for a slimming dish.

serves 4

2 large onions, cut into chunks
I large aubergine, cut into chunks
3 potatoes, scrubbed and cut into chunks
2 red peppers, seeded and cut into chunks
3 courgettes, cut into chunks
I head of garlic, cloves peeled and left whole
bunch of parsley, chopped
6–7 tablespoons olive oil
425 g can of chopped tomatoes

Put all the raw vegetables, the garlic and parsley into a large shallow casserole dish, mixing them
together and smoothing them into a flat layer.

Sprinkle with salt and pepper, then pour over the oil and add the tomatoes on top. Season again lightly.

Bake uncovered at 160°C/325°F/Gas Mark 3 for 2–3 hours, until the vegetables are tender.

CHUNKY OVEN-BAKED RATATOUILLE ★

This is a substantial ratatouille, which you can make even more filling, if you wish, by adding a drained can of white or red beans 10 minutes before it's cooked. You could cut the vegetables into smaller pieces, in which case they'll cook more quickly, so keep an eye on them.

serves 4

1 large red onion, cut into chunks
1 large courgette, cut into chunky pieces
1 large aubergine, cut into chunky pieces
2 red and 2 golden peppers,
   seeded and cut into chunks
450 g (1 lb) small tomatoes
   or large cherry tomatoes
4 garlic cloves, chopped
3 tablespoons olive oil
several sprigs of fresh basil

Preheat the oven to 240°C/475°F/Gas Mark 9.

Put all the vegetables and the garlic in a roasting tray or large shallow casserole dish, sprinkle with the oil and some salt and pepper, then mix with your hands so that they all get coated. Put into the oven and cook, uncovered, for 30–40 minutes, until the vegetables are browned at the edges, tender and smelling gorgeous. Tear the basil over the top and serve.

SPICY RATATOUILLE For a spicy version, stir 1–2 teaspoons of cumin seeds and/or 1–2 teaspoons of crushed coriander seeds in with the vegetables, and leave out the basil.

JUICY RATATOUILLE For a particularly juicy version, use a 425 g can of tomatoes in juice (organic, if possible) instead of the fresh tomatoes, adding them about 20 minutes before the end of the cooking time.

RED ONION AND GOAT'S CHEESE TART

This modern vegetarian classic is so unfailingly popular that it's worth the bit of trouble it takes to prepare, and you can do it in stages, which makes it practical.

serves 6

FOR THE PASTRY
115 g (4 oz) plain wholemeal flour
115 g (4 oz) plain white flour
115 g (4 oz) butter, cubed
3–4 tablespoons cold water

FOR THE FILLING
1 kg (2 lb 4 oz) red onions, peeled and thinly sliced
2 tablespoons olive oil
2 tablespoons sugar
3 tablespoons sherry
2 tablespoons red wine vinegar
350 g (12 oz) firm goat's cheese log, sliced

Cook the onions in the oil in a large saucepan, covered, for about 15 minutes until they're very tender, stirring every 5 minutes. They must be really soft.

Add the sugar, sherry and vinegar. Cook gently, uncovered, for about 30 minutes until thick and sticky with hardly any liquid left. Season and cool.

For the pastry, lightly blend the flours, butter and ½ teaspoon of salt in a food processor. Add the water and whiz to a soft dough. Roll out to fit a shallow 28–30 cm (11–12 in) flan tin. Trim. Prick the base, then cover with greaseproof paper and baking beans. Bake at 200°C/400°F/Gas Mark 6, for 15 minutes, remove the beans and paper and bake for a further 5 minutes.

Put the onion mixture into the flan. Cover with the goat's cheese. Put back into the oven for 20–30 minutes until the cheese has melted and browned.

ONION, TOMATO AND BASIL CRUSTLESS QUICHE ★

This is a delightful quiche replacement: you almost forget it hasn't any pastry. Don't turn your nose up at using dried basil if you can't get fresh; it may not have quite the flavour of fresh, but it's very good in this dish.

serves 4

2 onions, chopped
1 tablespoon olive oil
6 free-range eggs
3 tablespoons soya milk
2–3 good leaves of basil, torn, or a little dried basil
3 tomatoes, sliced

Preheat the oven to 200°C/400°F/Gas Mark 6.

Fry the onions in the oil in a covered pan for 10 minutes, until tender but not browned.

Whisk the eggs with the soya milk and season to taste.

Put the onion into a deep 22–23 cm (8–9 in) quiche dish or other suitable ovenproof dish. Season the onions, then pour the eggs on top. If you're using fresh basil, stir that in now. Season the tomato slices and arrange lightly all over the top. Season again and, if you're using dried basil, sprinkle a pinch over each tomato.

Bake for about 25 minutes, until risen up, golden brown and set in the centre – insert the point of a sharp knife or skewer to make sure there's no uncooked egg. Serve hot, warm or cold.

EGG FU YONG ★

This is quick and easy to make – and can be varied by adding ingredients such as sliced button mushrooms or canned water chestnuts. You can also make a very good vegan version by replacing the beaten eggs with tofu, as described.

serves 4

2 onions, sliced
1 green pepper, seeded and sliced
2 tablespoons olive oil
400 g (14 oz) beansprouts
2 garlic cloves, crushed
2 teaspoons grated fresh ginger
2 tablespoons tomato purée
2 tablespoons wine vinegar
2 teaspoons honey
2 tablespoons tamari or soy sauce
6 eggs, beaten, or 250g packet of tofu, drained and well mashed
4 tablespoons chopped fresh coriander

Fry the onion and green pepper in the oil in a large saucepan for 10 minutes, until tender.

Add the beansprouts, mix well, and cook for a further 3–4 minutes until they soften.

Stir in the garlic, ginger, tomato purée, wine vinegar, honey and tamari or soy sauce and cook for a minute or two.

Turn up the heat so that the juices are sizzling, then pour in the beaten eggs or, for the vegan version, the tofu. Turn the heat down a little and stir the mixture gently for a few minutes until the eggs have set or the tofu is heated through.

Check the seasoning, then stir in the coriander and serve at once.

GRATIN DAUPHINOISE WITH WILD MUSHROOMS

Serving this delicious gratin with a salad dressed in vinaigrette lowers the
GI, as does replacing some of the potato slices with celeriac – although
for a special treat it's unbeatable just as it is.

serves 6–8

50 g (2 oz) butter
500 g (1 lb 2 oz) wild mushrooms,
 cleaned and sliced
2 kg (4 lb 8 oz) potatoes
6 garlic cloves, crushed
freshly grated nutmeg
300 ml (½ pint) double cream
3 tablespoons truffle oil

Preheat the oven to 180°C/350°F/Gas Mark 4.

Heat three-quarters of the butter in a saucepan, add the mushrooms and cook for 5–10 minutes, until
the mushrooms are tender. If there's any liquid, strain it off and save it.

Slice the potatoes – which can be peeled or not, as you wish – as thinly as you can; a food processor
with a slicing attachment is great for this. Put the potato slices into a colander and rinse under the cold
tap to get rid of the excess starch.

Peel and chop the garlic and mix with the remaining butter. Use this butter to grease a large shallow
gratin dish generously. I use one that measures 24 × 30 cm (9½ × 12 in).

Layer half the potatoes into the dish and season well with salt, pepper and nutmeg. Spoon the
mushrooms on top, season again, then top with the remaining potatoes and season once more.

Pour the cream over the top, then fill the cream carton with any liquid that you strained from the
mushrooms, plus water to fill it to the top, and pour that over the potatoes, too.

Drizzle the truffle oil over the top and bake for 1½ hours, until you can easily insert a sharp knife into
the potatoes and the top is golden brown. Part of the joy of this dish is the contrast between the
crunchy top and the meltingly tender potato within. However, if the top seems to be getting too brown,
cover it with some foil, but remove it 10–15 minutes before the end of cooking to crisp the top.

You can make a vegan version of this dish using 600 ml (1 pint) of vegetable stock instead of the cream
and water.

QUICK AFTER-WORK MEALS

Golden Thai Curry (page 42)
Grilled Spiced Tofu with Peppers (page 148)
Lychees, Kiwis and Ginger (page 166)

Quick Grilled Mediterranean Vegetables (page 43)
Light and Creamy Hummus (page 88)
Buckwheat with Lemon and Herbs (page 132) or fluffy cooked quinoa

Spaghetti with Red Hot Sauce (page 67)
Green salad
Peach and Blueberry Compote (page 175)

KERALAN CURRY

This is a wonderful dish for a party – everyone loves it, and you can make it the day before. Serve it with Lemony Rice (page 137), Fresh Tomato and Coriander Chutney (page 70), mango chutney and some warm poppadums. For a lower-fat alternative to coconut milk, see the note on page 42.

serves 6

1 tablespoon oil
2 onions, chopped
4 carrots, sliced
1 baking potato, cut into 1 cm ($\frac{1}{2}$ in) cubes
1 small cauliflower, divided into small florets
250 g (9 oz) green beans, trimmed and halved
1 green chilli, seeded and chopped
1$\frac{1}{2}$ teaspoons ground coriander
1$\frac{1}{2}$ teaspoons ground cumin
1$\frac{1}{2}$ teaspoons ground turmeric
400 g can of coconut milk

FOR THE CURRY PASTE
1 beefsteak tomato, skinned and chopped
6 garlic cloves, crushed
3 knobs of fresh ginger, peeled and roughly chopped
1$\frac{1}{2}$ teaspoons fennel seeds
6 cloves
6 cardamom pods

Heat the oil in a large saucepan, add the onion and fry for 5 minutes. Then stir in the carrots, cover the pan, turn the heat down low and cook for 10 minutes. Add the potato, cover and cook gently for another 10 minutes, before adding the cauliflower, beans and chilli. Stir, cover and cook gently until all the vegetables are nearly tender, then stir in the coriander, cumin and turmeric and cook for a minute or two longer.

While the vegetables are cooking, make the curry paste. Put all the ingredients into a food processor and whiz to a purée.

Add the curry paste to the vegetables, stirring well, cook for 5–10 minutes, then pour in the coconut milk and salt to taste (approximately 1 tablespoon) and cook for a further minute or two until the coconut milk is hot. Serve immediately.

SPINACH CURRY (SAG BHAJI) ★

Iron-rich, slightly bitter, dark green spinach leaves, cooked with warming spices, make a wonderful side dish for curries. I particularly like them just with spoonfuls of Lentil Dal (page 109) and some sliced tomatoes.

serves 2–4

I onion, chopped
I tablespoon olive oil
2 garlic cloves, crushed
I tablespoon fresh ginger, grated
I teaspoon turmeric
I teaspoon ground coriander
500 g (I lb 2 oz) spinach leaves

Fry the onion in the oil in a large pan for 10 minutes, covered, until the onion is tender.

Add the garlic, ginger, turmeric and coriander. Stir for a few seconds over the heat, until they smell fragrant, then push in the spinach and stir it around as well as you can to get it coated with the spices.

Cover, then cook over a moderate heat for about 10 minutes, until the spinach is soft and much reduced in volume, stirring it from time to time. Season with salt and pepper and serve.

THE MAGIC OF TURMERIC Turmeric, the spice that gives curries their golden colour, and a staple ingredient in Eastern cookery, has been found to have remarkable therapeutic properties. Clinical studies have shown that not only does it help to prevent the formation of tumours in the body, giving protection from cancer, it also lowers cholesterol levels, helps to keep the blood thin, increases bile production and flow, and exerts a powerful anti-inflammatory action, which protects the stomach and eases irritable bowel syndrome. A pinch of turmeric a day really could keep the doctor away.

CABBAGE THORAN

This makes a very pleasant side dish for a selection of curries, or you can serve it as I usually do, with some simply cooked brown basmati rice and some Lentil Dal (page 109). Children like it because of the coconut, so it's a good way of getting them to eat their greens.

serves 2–4

1 onion, sliced
1 tablespoon olive oil
1 teaspoon mustard seeds
½ teaspoon turmeric
½ a cinnamon stick, broken
12 curry leaves or ½ teaspoon curry powder
225 g (8 oz) cabbage, shredded
50 g (2 oz) desiccated coconut

Fry the onion in the oil in a covered pan for about 7 minutes, until the onion is almost tender.

Add the mustard seeds, turmeric, cinnamon stick and curry leaves or powder. Stir for a few seconds, until they smell fragrant, then add the cabbage and coconut.

Stir well, then cover and leave to cook gently for about 10 minutes, until the cabbage is tender. Season with salt and pepper and serve.

TIME-SAVING WITH INDIAN MEALS A meal made up of a lot of different spicy dishes is a delight, but who has the time to make them all? One way of doing it is to make more than you need each time and save what's left. Curries keep very well for several days in the fridge and just go on getting better as the flavours blend. So by adding a new dish every day to serve with the others, you get a constantly evolving selection without much effort.

PASTA AND NOODLES

PASTA MADE WITH DURUM WHEAT, BUCKWHEAT NOODLES FROM JAPAN AND TRANSPARENT MUNG BEAN NOODLES ALL HAVE A LOW GI RATING. COMBINE THEM WITH PLENTY OF VEGETABLES, HERBS AND FLAVOURINGS AND, FOR PROTEIN, A SCATTERING OF STRONGLY FLAVOURED GRATED CHEESE, OR YOGURT AS A PUDDING, TO MAKE A PROPERLY BALANCED, HEALTH-GIVING, EASY AND DELICIOUS MEAL. THE IDEAL QUANTITY OF PASTA FOR A LOW-GI MEAL IS 75 G (3 OZ) DRY WEIGHT PER PERSON, OR 40 G (1½ OZ) IF YOU ARE SLIMMING.

SOBA NOODLES WITH GREEN SOYA BEANS

Cold noodles seem strange at first, but they are very popular in Japan, and once you try them like this they're quite addictive. I love them with a side dish of green soya beans, or edamame as they're known in Japan (there's a picture of them on page 29). You can buy these frozen from Oriental shops. Do try them if you can find them – suck the beans out of the pods into your mouth and discard the pods – but if you can't, the noodles are still very good on their own.

serves 4

250 g (9 oz) soba (or buckwheat) noodles
I packet of frozen green soya beans (edamame)
4 teaspoons sesame seeds
I tablespoon toasted sesame oil
I tablespoon mirin, apple juice concentrate
  or clear honey
I tablespoon rice vinegar
I tablespoon soy sauce
4 salad onions, cut into shreds

Bring two saucepans of water to the boil, a big one for the noodles and another for the soya beans. Cook the soba noodles for about 4 minutes, or according to the directions on the packet, and cook the soya beans for about the same amount of time, with some salt added to the water, until they are tender (you probably won't understand the packet directions unless you can read Japanese).

Meanwhile, toast the sesame seeds by stirring them in a small saucepan for a minute or two until they smell toasted and start to jump around the pan. Remove from the heat and tip them on to a plate so they don't go on cooking and get burnt and bitter.

Drain the noodles in a colander and rinse under the cold tap. Put them in a bowl, then pour in the sesame oil, mirin, apple juice concentrate or honey, the vinegar and soy sauce. Toss the noodles so they all get coated, then stir in the salad onions and toasted sesame seeds. Drain the soya beans and put into a bowl. Serve with the noodles.

CONCHIGLIE WITH BROCCOLI

This is a perfect example of the healthy low-GI way to eat pasta – with lots of tasty vegetables. The hot, tender, garlicky broccoli is excellent with the chewy pasta.

serves 2

700 g (1½ lb) broccoli florets
115 g (4 oz) conchiglie pasta
2 tablespoons olive oil
4 garlic cloves, sliced
½ teaspoon dried red chilli flakes
a little grated Parmesan-style cheese, to serve (optional)

Start the sauce. Halve or quarter the broccoli florets so they are all roughly the same size – not too big. Cook them in 2 cm (1 in) boiling water, with a lid on the pan, for 4–5 minutes or until tender. Drain.

Put a large saucepan of water on the stove and bring to the boil; put in the pasta and boil until al dente, following packet directions. Drain and return to the pan with 1 tablespoon of the olive oil. Season.

While the pasta is cooking, fry the garlic in 1 tablespoon of the oil in a saucepan, for 1 minute. Put in the chilli flakes and fry for a further 30 seconds or so, then add the drained broccoli and some salt and pepper. Cook gently, uncovered, for a few minutes until the broccoli has collapsed a bit, stirring from time to time.

Serve the pasta with the broccoli and a little cheese if liked.

SPAGHETTI WITH RED HOT SAUCE

This sauce is a brilliant scarlet, as warming to look at as it is to eat, with the sweetness of the pepper and the kick of the chilli. Serve with a big green salad.

serves 4

2 tablespoons olive oil
1 onion, chopped
1 red pepper, diced
425 g can of tomatoes in juice
1 garlic clove, chopped
½ teaspoon dried chilli flakes
250 g (9 oz) spaghetti
Parmesan cheese, flaked or grated, to serve (optional)

For the sauce, heat 1 tablespoon of the oil in a saucepan, add the onion, cover and cook gently for 5 minutes, then add the red pepper and cook for another 5 minutes. Pour in the tomatoes, chopping them a bit with the spoon, add the garlic and chilli flakes, stir and leave to cook, uncovered, for about 15 minutes, until thick. Season with salt and pepper.

Meanwhile, bring a big saucepan of water to the boil for the spaghetti. Add the spaghetti and cook according to the packet directions, but bite a piece a minute or so before the packet says it will be ready to make sure you get it nice and al dente. Drain the pasta and put it back into the still-warm pan.

If you're going to serve the sauce mixed with the pasta, add it now and season to taste (you don't need the rest of the oil). Alternatively, if you'd rather serve the sauce sitting on top of the pasta, swirl the pasta with the rest of the oil and some seasoning, then serve it out and spoon the sauce on top. Serve the cheese separately, if using.

NOODLES WITH STIR-FRIED VEGETABLES

The best noodles for this dish are Chinese transparent noodles made from mung beans, but actually this stir-fried mixture works with any long, thin pasta, even spaghetti. And if you're really pressed for time, try using a packet of frozen stir-fry vegetables instead of fresh ones.

serves 4

250 g (9 oz) transparent noodles
1 tablespoon toasted sesame oil
140 g (5 oz) baby sweetcorn, halved diagonally
140 g (5 oz) mangetout, halved vertically into shreds
4 salad onions, sliced
1 large red chilli, seeded and sliced
1 carrot, cut into thin shreds
225 g can of water chestnuts, drained
soy sauce
2 tablespoons coriander, chopped

Prepare the noodles according to the directions on the packet. This usually means putting them into a bowl, covering with boiling water and leaving to stand for 5 minutes.

Meanwhile, heat the oil in a large saucepan and add the sweetcorn, mangetout, salad onions, chilli, carrot and water chestnuts. Stir-fry for about 3 minutes, until the vegetables are heated through but still crunchy.

Season with a few drops of soy sauce and salt and pepper to taste. Stir in the chopped coriander and serve.

QUICK SALADS AND DRESSINGS

TOFU MAYONNAISE

This has the creaminess of traditional mayonnaise with only a tiny fraction of the calories, plus all the goodness and protein of tofu. A big spoonful of this turns a salad into a light main course. Drain a 250 g (9 oz) block of tofu, break it up roughly and put into a food processor with a crushed garlic clove, 1 teaspoon of Dijon mustard, the juice of half a lemon, and whiz to a thick, creamy consistency. If you want it thinner, you can add a little water or soya milk. Season with salt and freshly ground black pepper.

FRESH TOMATO AND CORIANDER CHUTNEY

This is what I love to serve with Indian curries and spicy food. All you do is cut up 225 g (8 oz) fresh tomatoes, season with salt and pepper, and mix with a tablespoon of chopped fresh coriander. Sometimes I squeeze a little lemon juice over or add a tablespoon of thinly sliced onion – a salad onion or an ordinary cooking onion. You can vary the herbs: fresh basil or mint is nice instead of the coriander. As an alternative, add a large, peeled, chopped avocado to the tomatoes, and use basil in place of the coriander. Season with salt and pepper and add a final squeeze of lemon juice.

MIDDLE EASTERN CARROT SALAD

A pile of freshly grated carrot is often included in Middle Eastern salad platters, and looks and tastes so vibrant that I can eat it just as it is. If it's juicy, and quite finely grated, I don't think it needs much dressing – a dash of vinaigrette maybe, or some Light Dressing (see opposite), or simply a squeeze of orange or lemon juice. You can add chopped fresh herbs – parsley, mint or chives – or chopped apple, thinly sliced onion or fennel, or raisins.

RAITA

This is really just thick yogurt with herbs or vegetables added. Don't make it too far in advance or it may go watery. Simply stir 2 tablespoons of chopped fresh coriander, mint or chives into 300 ml (½ pint) yogurt, or use half a peeled and diced cucumber (blotted on kitchen paper to take off some of the moisture), 1–2 shredded salad onions or a coarsely grated carrot.

LIGHT DRESSINGS

You can make a delicious, completely fat-free dressing using equal parts of a good soy sauce, lime juice and rice vinegar. Mix together and use like a vinaigrette. You could use lemon juice but the lime gives it an extra aroma; and you could sweeten it a little with a dash of honey or apple juice concentrate, if you wish. Or try a Light Vinaigrette: shake together in a screw-top jar equal parts of olive oil, freshly squeezed lemon juice, red wine vinegar and water, with salt, pepper and a spoonful of Dijon mustard. Store in the fridge; shake before use.

SPROUTED BEANS AND SEEDS

You can buy these, but they are also easy to make yourself. Just soak a couple of tablespoons of your chosen beans or seeds overnight: chick peas, green lentils, mung beans, alfalfa seeds and sunflower seeds all sprout well, or you can buy packets of sprouting mix at some health shops. Next day, rinse them and put into a jar with a piece of muslin secured over the top with an elastic band, or one of the special bean sprouting jars you can buy with a perforated lid. Rinse twice a day by filling the jar with water through the muslin/lid, shaking around and draining out. Keep the jar on its side, preferably in a dark place or covered with a cloth. The sprouts will appear in a couple of days and you can eat them in 3–4 days. Rinse first, then add to salads.

FUSILLI WITH UNCOOKED TOMATO AND BASIL SAUCE

I never tire of this classic, summery pasta dish. Made with fragrant summer tomatoes and basil, pale green unfiltered cold-pressed olive oil and some buttery chunks of avocado, it's a delight and takes virtually no time to prepare. It's lovely made with fusilli, but for a change I also make it with buckwheat pasta twists and the protein-rich, wheat-free soya parsley and garlic pasta twists you can find at specialist health food shops.

serves 2–3

200 g (7 oz) fusilli
450 g (1 lb) tomatoes, chopped
2 garlic cloves, crushed or finely chopped
2 good sprigs of fresh basil, torn
1 tablespoon olive oil
1 ripe avocado, peeled, stoned and cut into chunks

Bring a large saucepan of water to the boil and add the pasta. Cook according to the packet directions, but bite a piece a minute or so before the packet says it will be ready to make sure you get it nice and al dente.

Drain the pasta in a colander, then return it to the still-warm saucepan and add the tomatoes, garlic, basil, olive oil and salt and pepper to taste. Swirl it around, then stir in the avocado chunks and serve.

A spoonful of pesto makes a pleasant addition. Stir it in with the pasta before adding the tomatoes.

UNFILTERED COLD-PRESSED OLIVE OIL I adore this stuff – it's so green, so full of the flavour of olives. If you put some into a wide-necked jar or a bowl and chill it in the fridge for a few hours, it will become thick and you can then use it as a spread instead of butter – the purest and healthiest olive oil spread you could possibly get, and by far the best thing to put on your bread.

LINGUINE WITH PEPPERS, BASIL AND PECORINO

This is blissfully easy and very popular. You could include a few black olives as well, for piquancy.

serves 4

1 red pepper, halved and seeded
1 golden pepper, halved and seeded
250 g (9 oz) linguine or other pasta
1 tablespoon olive oil
1 garlic clove, crushed
3 or 4 sprigs of basil, torn
Pecorino cheese, flaked or grated, to serve

Preheat the grill. Put the peppers, cut-side down, on a grill pan and grill until the skin is blistered and blackened in places. Remove from the grill and leave until cool enough to handle, then strip off the skin (if you wish) and cut the peppers into strips.

Meanwhile, bring a big saucepan of water to the boil and add the pasta. Cook according to the packet directions, but bite a piece a minute or so before the packet says it will be ready to make sure you get it nice and al dente.

Drain the pasta in a colander, then return it to the still-warm saucepan with the olive oil, garlic, and salt and pepper to taste. Swirl it around, stir in the pepper strips and basil, then serve. Hand round the cheese separately.

For a vegan alternative, make exactly as described but serve without the cheese; an extra spoonful of good olive oil, added at the table, is a nice addition.

VEGETARIAN AND VEGAN CHEESES Many cheeses are now made with vegetarian rennet (instead of rennet made from animals' digestive juices), and these are usually labelled as such. However, some vegetarian cheeses do not advertise the fact, so it's worth asking. There is a vegetarian Parmesan, but if you like a good, strong flavour, you might prefer to use a traditionally made hard Pecorino, which is vegetarian. Vegan cheeses have improved enormously and can often be used instead of dairy cheese. I like the 'Cheddar-style' dairy-free slices.

PASTA AND NOODLES

PASTA WITH CHERRY TOMATOES AND ASPARAGUS

This is such an easy pasta dish. The 'sauce' makes itself under the grill while you cook the pasta. It's low in fat – and could be completely fat-free if you like. Serve with a crunchy green salad.

serves 4

300 g (10 oz) cherry tomatoes, stems removed
175 g (6 oz) asparagus tips
2 tablespoons olive oil
225 g (8 oz) pasta (I like to use fettuccine)
few sprigs of basil

Put a big saucepan of water on the stove to heat for the pasta. Set the grill to high.

Place the cherry tomatoes in a single layer in a grill pan. Brush the asparagus tips with half the olive oil, then cut the spears in half and put these in the grill pan, too. Put under the grill.

When the water comes to a rolling boil, add the pasta and cook for about 12 minutes, or according to the directions on the packet, but bite a piece a minute or so before the packet says it will be ready to make sure you get it nice and al dente. Drain in a colander, then return to the pan with the rest of the olive oil and salt and pepper to taste.

While the pasta is cooking, keep an eye on the asparagus and tomatoes; the tomatoes need to be on the point of collapse and the asparagus just tender to the point of a knife and perhaps tinged brown in places. Add the tomatoes and asparagus to the pasta, tear in some basil and serve.

For a fat-free version, grill the tomatoes as described (with no oil) but don't grill the asparagus; just throw this in with the pasta a couple of minutes before the pasta is cooked. Drain them together and then stir in the seasoning, tomatoes and basil as before.

PAPPARDELLE WITH AUBERGINE AND ARTICHOKES

This is a useful recipe because it uses mainly storecupboard ingredients to make an excellent fast meal. Serve with a big green salad.

serves 4

250 g (9 oz) pappardelle
4 tablespoons olive oil
1 onion, chopped
1 aubergine, diced
3–4 garlic cloves, chopped
1 jar of artichoke hearts
8 sun-dried tomatoes, roughly chopped
2 tablespoons capers, rinsed and drained
2 tablespoons pine nuts
small handful of basil leaves, torn
Parmesan cheese, flaked or grated (optional)

Put a big saucepan of water on the stove to heat for the pasta. When it comes to the boil, add the pasta and cook for about 12 minutes, or according to the directions on the packet, but bite a piece a minute or so before the packet says it will be ready to make sure you get it nice and al dente.

Meanwhile, heat 2 tablespoons of the oil in another pan and add the onion and aubergine. Cover and cook gently for 7 minutes, or until they are very nearly tender, then add the garlic and cook for a further 1–2 minutes. Drain the artichoke hearts and add to the aubergine mixture, along with the sun-dried tomatoes and capers.

Toast the pine nuts by putting them under a hot grill for a minute or two (watch carefully – they burn very quickly) or stirring them around in a dry saucepan over the heat until they're golden.

When the pasta is ready, drain it in a colander, then return it to the still-hot saucepan. Add the aubergine mixture and season well with salt and freshly ground black pepper. Serve on warmed plates, scattered with pine nuts and some torn basil leaves. Serve the Parmesan separately, if using.

PASTA TWIST, TOMATO AND MOZZARELLA BAKE

This is quick to make, and once it's all mixed together can be grilled and served straight away or kept ready for grilling or baking and serving later. It's a good dish for a crowd; just multiply everything up. I like to serve a crisp green salad with it.

serves 2

> **1 tablespoon olive oil**
> **1 onion, chopped**
> **1 garlic clove, chopped**
> **425 g can of tomatoes in juice**
> **140 g (5 oz) mozzarella cheese, drained and diced**
> **115 g (4 oz) fresh Parmesan or Pecorino cheese, grated**
> **175 g (6 oz) pasta twists (fusilli)**

Heat the oil in a saucepan, add the onion, cover and cook gently for 7 minutes, then add the garlic and tomatoes, chopping them a bit with the spoon. Stir and leave to cook, uncovered, for about 15 minutes, until thick, then remove from the heat and stir in the mozzarella, half the Parmesan or Pecorino and salt and pepper to taste.

Meanwhile, cook the pasta in a large saucepan of water according to the packet directions, but bite a piece a minute or so before the packet says it will be ready to make sure you get it nice and al dente. Drain the pasta, then add to the tomato mixture.

Pour into a shallow casserole dish and sprinkle with the rest of the Parmesan or Pecorino. Put under a hot grill for about 10 minutes until golden brown and bubbling.

You can make a vegan version by replacing the mozzarella with an extra tablespoon of olive oil and a handful of black olives, and topping the bake with grated vegan white Cheshire-style cheese.

GRILLED VEGETABLE LASAGNE

I must be honest, this is fiddly and a bit time-consuming to make, though
not difficult. I'm including it because it's a really useful dish that you can
prepare in advance for a crowd – and because everyone always asks for it!

serves 4

1–2 courgettes, halved or quartered lengthways
   and cut into 5 cm (2 in) lengths
1 red onion, cut into sixths
1 aubergine, cut into chunky pieces
1 tablespoon olive oil
1 tablespoon fresh lemon juice
1 red and 1 yellow pepper, seeded and cut into strips
12 black olives
425 g can of artichoke hearts, drained and halved
225 g (8 oz) lasagne sheets
small bunch of basil
425 g can of chopped tomatoes, in juice
3 × 115 g (4 oz) mozzarella cheese, drained and sliced
1 × quantity **Light and Creamy White Sauce** (see page 147)
115 g (4 oz) Pecorino cheese, grated

Heat the grill to high. Put the courgette, onion and aubergine chunks on to a tray that will fit under your grill, add the olive oil, lemon juice and a sprinkling of salt, and move the vegetables around so that they all get coated. I use my hands for this.

Add the pepper pieces to the tray – these don't need oiling, as they cook perfectly without. Grill for about 20 minutes, or until the vegetables are tender and browned in places, stirring them often. Stir in the black olives and artichoke hearts and set aside.

To assemble the dish, dip sheets of lasagne into cold water to soak on both sides, then place a single layer to cover the base of a shallow casserole dish. Put half the vegetables on top, followed by a layer of basil leaves, half the tomatoes, a good seasoning of salt and pepper, half the mozzarella, another layer of lasagne, half the cream sauce and half the Pecorino. Repeat the layers – vegetables, basil, tomatoes, seasoning, mozzarella, lasagne and a final layer of cream sauce. Finish with the rest of the Pecorino.

Bake at 200°C/400°F/Gas Mark 6 for about 30 minutes, or until golden brown, bubbling and smelling gorgeous.

BEANS AND LENTILS

BEANS AND LENTILS – PULSES – ARE WONDERFUL: RICH IN PROTEIN AND THE KIND OF CARBOHYDRATE YOU NEED FOR STEADY BLOOD SUGAR AND SUSTAINED ENERGY, ALONG WITH MANY OTHER VALUABLE NUTRIENTS. THEY'RE SIMPLE TO USE, AS THE FOLLOWING RECIPES WILL DEMONSTRATE. APART FROM QUICK-COOKING LENTILS, WHICH ARE AS EASY TO PREPARE AS PASTA, I'VE USED CANNED BEANS IN MOST OF THE RECIPES; I'VE ALSO GIVEN DRIED BEAN/CANNED BEAN EQUIVALENT QUANTITIES (SEE PAGE 82), IN CASE YOU WANT TO HAVE A GO WITH DRIED BEANS.

PREPARING DRIED BEANS AND LENTILS

Make sure the beans and lentils are fresh when you buy them. Although they have superb keeping qualities, they do dry out over time. Be especially selective with dried chick peas, which can take for ever to cook if they're old. It's worth spending a bit more and getting top-quality ones – try Spanish food shops.

Soaking
All dried beans, with the exception of lentils, need soaking before you cook them. You have two options: the long, cold soak or the short, hot soak.

For the long, cold soak, cover the beans with plenty of cold water and leave to soak for 8 hours, or overnight.

For the short, hot soak, put the beans into a roomy saucepan, cover with water as before, and heat. Boil for 2 minutes, then remove from the heat and leave to stand, covered, for 1 hour.

You can soak lentils too, if you wish, but it's not necessary. They'll just cook a little more quickly. All you need to do is put them into a pan, cover with water – use the amount specified in the recipe if given, otherwise cover them with their height again – bring to the boil and simmer until tender, 20–50 minutes depending on the type (see opposite).

Cooking
After soaking, drain the beans in a colander, rinse under the cold tap, put them back into a saucepan and cover with their height again in fresh water. Bring to the boil and let them boil hard, uncovered, for 10 minutes to destroy any enzymes that could cause stomach upsets. Then let them simmer gently until tender (see opposite), or pressure-cook, which reduces cooking times by two-thirds.

If you're preparing a recipe using soaked but uncooked beans, be careful about what other ingredients you include. Salt and salty stocks, as well as acidic ingredients such as tomatoes, and some spices, will cause the outside of the beans to toughen and prevent them from cooking properly. It's best to add these flavourings after the beans have softened.

Freezing
Cooked pulses freeze well. I find it convenient to cook 500 g (1 lb 2 oz) dried beans, then drain them and freeze in roughly 225 g (8 oz) portions, which is approximately the weight of the drained contents of a 425 g can of beans; 500 g (1 lb 2 oz) dried beans yields 5 portions.

Dried bean and canned bean equivalents
It's easy to convert a recipe from dried beans to canned beans and vice versa: 100 g (3½ oz) dried beans is equivalent to a 425 g can of beans, which, when drained, weighs about 225 g (8 oz).

Making beans digestible

There's no getting away from it – beans and lentils do give some people wind. Pulses are so nutritious and delicious that it's a pity not to eat them because of this. I rather like Nigel Slater's comment: 'So, beans give you wind. And what is wrong with that?' However, if this is a problem for you, it may be that all you need to do is add more salt to your dishes, because pulses produce magnesium in the gut, hence the wind, and salt, potassium or something acidic like cider vinegar or fresh lemon juice, neutralizes it. You can also try adding plenty of spices – fennel seed, or almost any you fancy – for the same effect; that's one of the reasons Indian pulse recipes contain them. Rinsing the pulses at every stage – after soaking, after bringing to the boil and after cooking – can also help, as might cooking them with the lid off the pan. You may find you can tolerate some pulses better than others – and if you persevere, you could well find your body gradually adjusts and the problem eases.

COOKING TIMES

Pulses, soaked unless stated	Cooking time
Black beans	1¼–1½ hours
Butter beans	1¼–1½ hours
Cannellini beans	1¼–1½ hours
Chick peas	1–3 hours*
Flageolet beans	30 mins
Haricot beans	1 hour
Lentils, brown or green, unsoaked	50–60 mins
Lentils, Puy, unsoaked	40–45 mins
Lentils, split red, unsoaked	15–20 mins
Mung beans, unsoaked	35–45 mins
Mung bean dal (moong dal), unsoaked	15–20 mins
Red kidney beans	1¼–1½ hours
Soya beans	4 hours

*Some recipes suggest adding a pinch of bicarbonate of soda to chick peas at the beginning of cooking to help them to soften. This does destroy some of the B vitamins, though, and I prefer to be patient and cook them for a bit longer.

LENTIL AND VEGETABLE SOUP ★

Here, for a change, is an English-style lentil soup, and very comforting it is too. This makes a huge pot so you can keep some in the fridge or freeze it. But by all means halve the quantities if you wish.

serves 10

2 onions, chopped
2–3 carrots, cut into small dice
2 celery sticks, cut into small dice
1 small leek, chopped
2 tablespoons olive oil
500 g (1 lb 2 oz) split red lentils
250 ml can sweetcorn (no added sugar)
2 tablespoons tamari or soy sauce
1–2 tablespoons freshly squeezed lemon juice

Fry the onion, carrots, celery and leek in the oil in a large saucepan, covered, for 10 minutes, until beginning to soften, stirring often.

Add the lentils and 2.5 litres (4 pints) of water. Bring to the boil, then leave to simmer gently for 15–20 minutes until the lentils are pale and soft.

Remove 2–3 cupfuls of the soup and blend the rest, roughly, in a food processor or with a stick blender. Put the reserved cupfuls of soup back.

Add the sweetcorn, tamari or soy sauce and lemon juice, salt and pepper – white pepper is nice in this – to taste.

CURRIED LENTIL AND VEGETABLE SOUP If you want to spice it up for a change, try adding 1–2 tablespoons of curry powder and 2 tablespoons of tomato purée.

LEEK, CHICK PEA AND SAFFRON SOUP ★

This is such a lovely soup. It's very quick and easy to make, looks
beautiful – shredded leeks and parsley, white and green in a clear golden
broth studded with plump chick peas and flecked with deep orange
saffron stamens – and tastes clean and light, yet at the same time
warming and satisfying.

serves 4

> ½ **tablespoon olive oil**
> **250 g (9 oz) leeks, finely sliced**
> **a good pinch of saffron strands**
> **425 g can of chick peas**
> **2 tablespoons parsley, roughly chopped**

Heat the oil in a large saucepan and add the leeks. Stir gently so that they all get coated with the oil,
then cover and leave to cook for 4–5 minutes, but don't let them brown.

Add the saffron, chick peas and 600 ml (1 pint) water. Bring to the boil, then turn the heat down and
leave to simmer gently for 5–10 minutes, until the leeks are tender.

Stir in the chopped parsley, season and serve.

LEEK, CHICK PEA AND TURMERIC SOUP WITH LEMON Same colour,
different flavour – and cheaper. It's also particularly health-giving because of the protective properties
of turmeric (see page 60). Just add ½ teaspoon of turmeric instead of the saffron and stir in the juice
of 1 lemon with the parsley.

PISTOU ★

A fast and easy version of a favourite Provençal stew. Very, very evocative of France – a bowlful of this and I'm practically there.

serves 3–4

2 large onions, chopped
140 g (5 oz) sugarsnap or mangetout peas
3–4 courgettes, sliced
6 tomatoes (plum, if available), roughly chopped
4 garlic cloves, chopped
2 × 240 g cans of white haricot or cannellini beans
2 teaspoons vegetable bouillon powder

FOR THE PISTOU PURÉE
6 garlic cloves
2 tomatoes
handful of basil leaves
4 tablespoons olive oil

Put all the vegetables into a large saucepan with the garlic and the beans, together with their liquid. Pour in 600 ml (1 pint) water, sprinkle in the bouillon powder, 1 teaspoon of salt and a good grinding of black pepper and leave to simmer gently for about 30 minutes, until the vegetables are very tender.

Meanwhile, make the pistou purée. Put the cloves of garlic into a food processor and whiz to chop, then add the tomatoes and basil and whiz again. When they're chopped, add the oil and whiz again.

Stir the pistou purée into the pan of vegetables, cook for a couple of minutes, then serve.

VEGETABLE BOUILLON POWDER Vegetable bouillon powder has become a real culinary star, and is stocked in most health-food shops and supermarkets. Just mix with water, following the packet instructions, to make stock with an almost home-made flavour.

DIPS, PÂTÉS AND SPREADS

LENTIL AND BLACK OLIVE PÂTÉ

Whiz together the drained contents of a 425 g can of green or Puy lentils, a small crushed garlic clove, 4 sun-dried tomatoes, 120–175 g (4½–6 oz) stoned black olives, and the juice of half a lemon. Season with freshly ground black pepper, and salt, if necessary – very little is needed as the olives are already salty. For maximum flavour with minimum calories, try sun-dried tomatoes soaked for 10 minutes before use, and decrease the quantity of olives.

LIGHT AND CREAMY HUMMUS

Drain a 425 g can of chick peas, reserving the liquid. Whiz the chick peas in a food processor with 1 tablespoon of olive oil, 2 garlic cloves, 2 tablespoons of freshly squeezed lemon juice, 1 teaspoon of ground cumin and a little salt, until very smooth, adding a bit of the reserved chick pea liquid if necessary. Add 1–4 tablespoons of tahini (for a slimming version, leave this out) and whiz again until gloriously smooth and creamy, adding more of the liquid as you go – you probably won't need it all. Stop when you reach your desired consistency. Serve in a bowl, or spread it out on a plate and sprinkle the top with some paprika. You could also drizzle some olive oil over the top and decorate with a few olives, depending on what you're having with it.

TOFU SPREAD

This tastes rich and creamy, like a dairy-free version of garlic and herb cream cheese. Drain a 250 g packet of tofu, break it up roughly with your fingers and put it into a food processor with several sprigs of flat-leaf parsley, a small crushed garlic clove, a squeeze of lemon juice and some salt and pepper. Whiz until creamy. Check the seasoning, adding more salt, pepper and lemon juice if needed, then stir in 1 tablespoon of chopped chives or a finely chopped salad onion.

AVOCADO DIP

This is avocado at its simplest and creamiest, almost like green mayonnaise or butter. Halve, stone and peel a large, ripe avocado. Cut into rough chunks and whiz to a smooth cream in a food processor with 1 tablespoon of fresh lime or lemon juice, a few drops of tabasco and some salt and pepper to taste. For more texture, mash the avocado and feel free to add other ingredients: chopped tomatoes, chilli or coriander, for example.

MEDITERRANEAN BEAN PÂTÉ

This is very quick and easy to make and full of sunny flavours. Put the contents of a 425 g can of cannellini beans into a food processor with the juice of half a lemon, 3–4 sun-dried tomatoes (try the ones you soak for 10 minutes before use) and a small handful of stoned black olives, and whiz to a thick, chunky purée. Season with salt and pepper and tear some fresh basil leaves over the top. This is great in sandwiches, as a dip with crudités or on a plate with salad leaves and ripe tomatoes for a light meal.

BABA GANOOJ (AUBERGINE DIP)

This delectable, addictive, pale smoky cream is wonderful with crudités, warm bread or salad. Prick 3 aubergines in several places, then put them on a shelf in a hot oven (grid-style rather than a solid shelf), or arranged on the stove-top over gas burners (watch carefully if you choose this method) or under a very hot grill. For best results, the skins of the aubergines need to be well charred. This takes 25–30 minutes; you'll have to turn them frequently (with tongs). Cool, then peel off the charred skin – it will come off easily in long strips. Whiz the aubergine to a pale cream with 2 crushed garlic cloves, 3 tablespoons of tahini or plain low-fat yogurt, 3 tablespoons of olive oil and 3 tablespoons of lemon juice. Season with salt and pepper to taste, and add more lemon juice, if necessary.

BEAN SALADE NIÇOISE ★

This is a lovely salad, which always makes me think of holidays and sunshine. I love it for lunch, but it's also good as a starter, in which case it is enough for four.

serves 2–4

250 g (9 oz) thin French beans
400 g can of flageolet or haricot beans
250 g (9 oz) tomatoes, plum if available
few sprigs of basil
handful of black olives

FOR THE MUSTARD DRESSING
1 teaspoon Dijon mustard
$\frac{1}{2}$ a garlic clove, crushed
1 tablespoon red wine vinegar or cider vinegar
3 tablespoons olive oil

Trim the French beans – I like to take off the tops and leave the little curly 'tails'. Cook them in boiling water for 4–6 minutes, or until tender but still crunchy. Drain in a colander and cool under the cold tap. Drain again.

While they're cooking, drain and rinse the flageolet or haricot beans, cut the tomatoes into chunky pieces, tear the basil and put them all into a bowl, along with the olives. Add the French beans and season with salt and a little pepper.

For the dressing, put the mustard, garlic, vinegar and a little salt into a bowl and mix with a fork or small whisk, then gradually whisk in the oil. Season.

Add half the dressing to the salad and toss so that it's all glossy, then heap it onto plates or a serving dish and drizzle the rest of the dressing over and around. Grind over some more pepper and serve.

LENTIL AND CUMIN CAKES ★

There's something comforting and almost stodge-like about these; they're a bit like a bread you can really fill up on when eating low GI. Children love them. You can also form the mixture into a loaf shape instead of individual cakes. Serve with minty Raita (page 71).

makes about 16

250 g (9 oz) red lentils
1 onion, chopped
2 garlic cloves, chopped
2 teaspoons cumin seeds
olive oil for greasing
3–4 tablespoons gram flour (see page 106), for coating

Put the lentils into a saucepan with 500 ml (18 fl oz) water and bring to the boil, then cook gently for about 15 minutes, until the lentils are soft and pale gold and no water remains. Remove from the heat, cover and leave for 10–15 minutes to continue to cook and dry in the residual heat.

Meanwhile, in another saucepan, fry the onion, garlic and cumin gently in 1 tablespoon of the oil, for 7–8 minutes, until the onion is tender. Add the onion mixture to the lentils, mashing them with a wooden spoon. Season with plenty of salt and pepper to taste.

Preheat the oven to 200°C/400°F/Gas Mark 6. Brush a baking sheet with olive oil.

Put some of the gram flour onto a plate. Take ping-pong-ball-sized pieces of the lentil mixture, drop them into the gram flour, scatter with more gram flour and form into small, flat cakes, pressing them together firmly, or form into a loaf shape.

Put the cakes or the loaf on the oiled baking sheet, then turn them over so the tops are coated in oil. Bake the cakes for about 25 minutes, a loaf for about 45 minutes, turning them halfway through.

CHICK PEA, TOMATO AND CORIANDER SALAD ★

You can make this filling and nutritious snack in about five minutes. I like
to scoop it up with crisp Little Gem lettuce leaves, but you could pack it
into a pitta bread if you want to make it more filling.

serves 2

425 g can of chick peas, drained
4 tomatoes, chopped
I salad onion, chopped
I small garlic clove, crushed
squeeze of lemon juice
few sprigs of fresh coriander, chopped
drizzle of extra virgin olive oil (optional)

Mix all the ingredients together, and drizzle with the olive oil, if using.

FRENCH WHITE BEAN AND HERB SALAD Use a can of cannellini, haricot or
flageolet beans instead of the chick peas. Leave out the tomatoes, and instead of the coriander use
2–3 tablespoons of chopped summer herbs – parsley makes a good base, plus a little of anything else
available that takes your fancy: mint, tarragon, lovage, fennel, rosemary, thyme.

PUY LENTIL SALAD Follow the French White Bean and Herb Salad recipe, using either a can of
Puy lentils instead of the white beans, or 115 g (4 oz) dried Puy lentils cooked as described on pages 82–83.

THAI BEANCAKES WITH SWEET RED PEPPER SAUCE ★

Well, I thought, people make Thai crabcakes, so why not use the same flavourings to make Thai beancakes? It works.

serves 4 as a starter, 2 as a light meal

425 g can of cannellini beans
1 large salad onion, chopped
packet or small handful of coriander leaves, roughly chopped
2 teaspoons red Thai paste
1 dried lime leaf, crumbled, stem discarded
1 tablespoon gram flour (see page 106)
1–2 tablespoons olive oil
lime wedges, to serve

FOR THE RED PEPPER DIPPING SAUCE
1 red pepper
pinch of dried chilli flakes
1 tablespoon apple juice concentrate
1 teaspoon rice vinegar or cider vinegar

Start with the sauce. Using a potato peeler, remove as much of the shiny skin of the pepper as you can, although there's no need to be too fussy. Then halve, seed and finely chop the pepper. Put into a saucepan with the chilli flakes, the apple juice concentrate and vinegar and simmer, uncovered, for about 15 minutes, or until the pepper is tender. Season with salt and pepper.

Drain the beans in a sieve, then rinse under the cold tap. Blot thoroughly with kitchen paper so they're fairly dry. Then put into a food processor with the salad onion, coriander, red Thai paste, lime leaf and some salt and freshly ground black pepper and whiz briefly until you have a chunky purée that clings together.

Divide the mixture into four – or, if you're serving them as a starter and have the patience, eight – form into flat cakes and coat with the gram flour. Warm the olive oil in a frying pan and fry the cakes on both sides until golden. Serve immediately with the dipping sauce and lime wedges.

ASIAN SOYA BEANS ★

Soya beans are highly nutritious, as are products made from them, such as tofu, tempeh and miso. Produced in the traditional way with lengthy fermentation, they are, I believe, a safe and healthy addition to our diet. See pages 82–83 for how to cook soya beans, or use canned ones if you can find them, or substitute canned haricot beans, which are also delicious, though less protein-rich.

serves 4

2 onions, sliced
1 green pepper, seeded and sliced
2 tablespoons olive oil
2 garlic cloves, crushed
2 teaspoons grated fresh ginger
200 g (7 oz) soya beans, soaked, cooked and drained, or 2 × 410 g cans, drained
4 tablespoons tamari or soy sauce
2 tablespoons freshly squeezed lime juice
4 tablespoons chopped fresh coriander

Fry the onion and green pepper in the oil in a covered saucepan for 10 minutes, until tender.

Stir in the garlic and ginger and cook for a minute or two, then add the soya beans and tamari or soy sauce, and bubble over the heat for a minute or two.

Remove from the heat and stir in the lime juice and coriander.

Serve hot, warm or cold.

SOYA NUTS You can buy these, but they are also very easy to make. Soak soya beans overnight then drain and blot dry. Spread them out in a single layer on a baking sheet and bake for 20 minutes at 180°C/350°F/Gas Mark 4. Stir them, then bake for a further 20–25 minutes, stirring every 5 minutes, or until golden brown and crisp. Sprinkle with 1–2 teaspoons olive oil and onion salt, garlic salt or sea salt to taste. Store in a jar or airtight container.

GREEK BUTTER BEANS ★

Have you eaten these, or something similar, at a taverna by the harbourside on a Greek island some warm summer's evening, the air full of the scent of wild thyme and the sound of cicadas? Forgive me for getting carried away… Anyway, this is a quick version of the dish, using canned butter beans and sun-dried tomato purée instead of hours of slow cooking. It gives similar results, but no taverna or harbour lights – sorry. These are useful for serving with all kinds of things: they turn a bowl of leafy salad into a lunch; or they're great served alongside some fluffy grains, or scooped up with crusty bread.

serves 2–4

I onion, finely chopped
I tablespoon olive oil
I garlic clove, sliced
425 g can of butter beans (in salted water, not sweetened), drained
I tablespoon sun-dried tomato purée
juice of ½ a lemon
fresh parsley, thyme, basil or dill chopped

Fry the onion in the oil for 5 minutes, add the garlic and fry for a further 5 minutes.

Stir in the butter beans, sun-dried tomato purée, lemon juice, and salt and pepper to taste. If you use good-quality sun-dried tomato purée, it doesn't need any more cooking. Remove from the heat and stir in some chopped parsley, thyme, basil or dill. Let it stand for as long as possible for the flavours to develop. Serve warm or cold, as you like.

SLOW-COOK BLACK BEANS ★

Although I'm a great one for saving time by using canned beans, there are certain recipes that I really love to make with dried beans, and this is one of them. It really isn't any trouble – I just do a 'quick soak' rather than overnight, and then you just leave them to cook. It is deeply satisfying food that everyone loves, and one of those dishes that tastes even better when re-heated the next day. This is a good dish for slimming if you avoid the soured cream, avocado and any starchy accompaniments.

serves 4–6

500 g (1 lb 2 oz) black beans
2 large onions, chopped
2 tablespoons olive oil
1 tablespoon cumin seeds
6 garlic cloves, chopped
juice of 1 lemon or lime

TO SERVE
142 ml carton soured cream (optional)
bunch of fresh coriander, roughly chopped
1–2 big red chillies, sliced, with or without seeds
1 avocado, chopped (optional)
hot cooked rice, bread or tortilla chips (optional)

Put the beans into a large pan and cover with cold water to about 5 cm (2 in) above them. Soak overnight or boil for 2 minutes, then leave to stand for 1 hour (see page 82). Drain, add enough fresh water to cover the beans, bring to the boil and let them bubble hard for 10 minutes, then turn down the heat and leave to cook for 1¼–1½ hours, or until the beans are really tender, adding a bit more water if necessary.

Meanwhile, fry the onions in the oil for 10 minutes. Add the cumin and garlic and cook for another 2 minutes. Set aside.

When the beans are done, stir in the onions. Then take out about a quarter of the mixture and mash thoroughly or purée in a food processor. Put back with the rest of the beans and stir well, adding more water if necessary, the lemon or lime juice and plenty of salt and pepper.

Reheat, then top with a swirl of soured cream, if using, and a scattering of coriander, chilli and avocado, if using, or put these toppings into bowls along with the rice, bread or whatever else is on offer and let people help themselves. I like a leafy salad with a mustardy dressing, too.

BEST-EVER CHILLI ★

This is quick and easy to make, filling, totally healthy, cheap and very tasty. It's particularly good served over big potatoes that have been baked until their skins are really crisp – they need to go into a hot oven (230°C/450°F/ Gas Mark 8) 1–1½ hours before you want to eat – or, for a low-GI option, I like a crunchy green salad or some cooked broccoli with it.

serves 3–4

1 onion, chopped
1 large red pepper, seeded and chopped
2 garlic cloves, finely chopped
1 mild red chilli, seeded and finely chopped, or red chilli flakes, to taste
1 tablespoon olive oil
1 teaspoon ground coriander
425 g can of green lentils, drained
425 g can of red kidney beans, drained
425 g can of chopped tomatoes

TO SERVE
bunch of fresh coriander, roughly chopped
142 ml carton soured cream (optional)
1 avocado, chopped (optional)

To make the chilli, fry the onion, red pepper, garlic and chilli in the oil in a largish saucepan, covered, for 15–20 minutes, or until the vegetables are tender. Stir them from time to time to prevent them sticking.

Add the ground coriander, lentils, red kidney beans and tomatoes and mix well. Leave to simmer gently for 10 minutes, season, then serve with your chosen accompaniments and garnishes. If you're slimming, you can eat as much of this as you like so long as you go easy on the soured cream and avocado, and avoid starchy accompaniments.

VEGETABLE TEMPURA

Crisp, golden tempura make a lovely treat, and these are easy to make and quite nutritious, since gram flour is used in the batter. Serve, Oriental-style, with a dipping sauce and a little pile of grated raw turnip or daikon (which is said to help digest the oil), or with Tartare Sauce (see page 146) for a Western approach.

serves 4 as a starter, 2 as a main course

rapeseed oil for deep-frying
115 g (4 oz) gram flour (see page 106)
115 g (4 oz) white self-raising flour or arrowroot (see page 159)
1 teaspoon baking power, or 2 teaspoons if you're using arrowroot
½ teaspoon salt
300 ml (½ pint) ice-cold fizzy water
450 g (1 lb) assorted vegetables, in bite-size pieces: broccoli florets, mangetout, fresh beans, red onion, red pepper, asparagus spears, salad onions

FOR THE ACCOMPANIMENTS
1 tablespoon fresh ginger, grated
1 tablespoon soy sauce
1 tablespoon mirin, apple juice concentrate or honey
1 tablespoon rice vinegar
piece of daikon or 1 turnip, peeled and grated
sprinkling of sesame seeds

Heat the oil for deep-frying.

First make the dipping sauce: squeeze the ginger with your fingers over a small bowl to catch the golden juice. Discard the rest of the ginger and mix the soy sauce, mirin, apple juice concentrate or honey, and the rice vinegar with the ginger juice. Set aside, along with the grated daikon or turnip in another small bowl, garnished with a sprinkling of sesame seeds.

Put the gram flour into a bowl with the self-raising flour or arrowroot, baking powder and salt. Pour in the fizzy water, beating all the time – some little lumps don't matter for tempura batter.

When the oil is hot enough to sizzle and form bubbles when you dip a wooden chopstick or the handle of a wooden spoon into it, start dipping the vegetables into the batter to coat them, then dropping them into the oil. Don't do too many at once – just enough to cover the surface of the oil. Fry for about 4 minutes, flipping them over if the tops seem to be less golden, then remove from the oil with a slotted spoon and drain on kitchen paper. Continue with another batch until all the vegetables are done, then serve immediately with your chosen accompaniments.

PIZZA BAKE ★

This is a novel way to enjoy the rich flavours of pizza. Creamy puréed or mashed beans are topped with fried onions, tomatoes, peppers, olives, herbs, grated cheese and any other flavourings you fancy and baked until golden and sizzling. Quick to make and scrumptious to eat, it's also great with a salad, such as Little Gem, Chicory and Watercress on page 37, for extra crunch.

serves 4

2 large onions, chopped
2 tablespoons olive oil
3 × 410 g cans butterbeans, drained
400 g can tomatoes, drained and chopped
1 tablespoon Italian seasoning or oregano
1 small red pepper, seeded and thinly sliced
handful of black olives
50 g (2 oz) finely grated strong Cheddar

Preheat the oven to 200°C/400°F/Gas Mark 6.

Fry the onion in 1 tablespoon of the oil in a covered pan for about 10 minutes, until tender and beginning to turn golden.

Purée the butterbeans with half the onions, using a food processor or stick blender, or mash them well. Add about 3 tablespoons of water to make a consistency like mashed potatoes. Season.

Oil a baking sheet or shallow roasting tin with the rest of the oil. Spread the butterbean mixture evenly over it to a thickness of about 1 cm (½ in), to form a 'cake'.

Mix the rest of the onions with the tomatoes, Italian seasoning or oregano and salt and pepper. Spread over the top of the bean 'cake', then top evenly with the red pepper, olives and cheese.

Bake for 20–30 minutes, until golden brown. It won't cut into neat pieces – use a spatula to serve it out onto warmed plates.

SPECIAL MEALS

SUMMER BARBECUE

Lentil and Black Olive Pâté (page 88) with crudités
Oatcakes (page 131)
Tofu and Mushroom Skewers (page 145)
Cumin-roasted Sweet Potatoes (page 46)
Tempeh Burgers (page 151) with Tartare Sauce (page 146)
Little Gem, Chicory and Watercress Salad (page 37)
Lemon Cake (page 184)
Summer Berry Compote (page 175)

DRINKS PARTY

Marinated Olives (page 38)
Vegetarian Sushi (page 122)
Avocado Dip (page 89) with crudités
Deep-fried Tofu and Hijiki Balls (page 160)
Mini Chocolate Brownies topped with strawberries (page 187)

LITTLE PROVENÇAL PANCAKES

Make these pancakes small for a brilliant and easy first course, or larger, as a wrap, which is great for snacks.

makes about 16 little pancakes

225 g (8 oz) or 8 heaped tablespoons chick pea or gram flour (see below)
1 teaspoon salt
1 teaspoon baking powder
2 teaspoons cumin seeds
a little olive oil for frying
handful of fresh coriander, chopped

FOR THE SALSA TOPPING
1 beefsteak tomato, fairly finely chopped
2 salad onions, chopped
1 tablespoon lemon juice

Measure out 300–450 ml (10–16 fl oz) water and set aside. Sift the gram flour into a bowl with the salt and baking powder. Add the cumin seeds, then start pouring in the water, stirring all the time. Once you've got a thickish paste, stop pouring and beat to remove all the lumps, or as many as you can, then go on stirring the water into the paste until you've got a consistency like pouring cream.

To make the salsa, mix together all the ingredients and set aside.

To fry the little pancakes, warm 1 teaspoon of olive oil in a frying pan, then pour in a good tablespoonful of batter to make a little pancake. Put another in beside it, leaving some space between them. When the base looks set and little holes are appearing on top, flip each pancake over with a palette knife and cook the other side. Keep them warm while you repeat the process to make the rest, then top each with a spoonful of salsa and some chopped coriander and eat immediately, while they're light and fragrant.

CHICK PEA OR GRAM FLOUR This is a light golden flour which has all the nutrients of chick peas and a low glycaemic index rating. It makes beautiful pancakes and can be used to thicken bean mixtures. You can also use it to coat fritters, either as it is, instead of flour, or mixed to a thin paste with water and used instead of beaten egg: dip the fritters into this then into more chick pea flour or breadcrumbs before frying.

COURGETTE KOFTAS

Serve these crisp and tasty morsels with this sauce – or with Fresh Tomato and Coriander Chutney (page 70) – as a starter, or add some hot cooked rice to make a light main course.

serves 4 as a starter, 2 as a main course

750 g (1 lb 10 oz) courgettes, grated
1 medium onion, very finely chopped
115 g (4 oz) gram flour (see page 106)
1 teaspoon red pepper flakes
½ teaspoon baking powder
1 teaspoon salt
3 tablespoons fresh coriander or mint, chopped
rapeseed oil, for frying

FOR THE SAUCE
2 teaspoons olive oil
1 onion, finely chopped
2 garlic cloves, crushed
2 teaspoons fresh ginger, grated
6 fresh curry leaves or ½ teaspoon curry powder
2 beefsteak tomatoes, chopped

First make the sauce. Heat the oil in a saucepan, add the onion and fry gently for 5 minutes, then add the garlic, ginger and curry leaves or powder and cook for a further 5 minutes, until the onion is tender. Add the tomatoes and leave to cook gently for about 10 minutes, until the tomatoes are softened, then add salt and pepper to taste.

While the sauce is simmering, make the koftas. Squeeze the excess juice from the courgettes, then mix with all the other ingredients, except the oil.

Just before you're ready to serve the meal – because koftas are best eaten hot, sizzling and crisp – heat 1 cm (½ in) rapeseed oil in a deep frying pan or wok.

Drop straggly, slightly flattened, walnut-sized chunks of the kofta mixture into the oil and fry for 2–3 minutes, or until they're brown on one side, then flip them over and cook the other side. Make sure they're nice and brown and crisp, then lift out with a slotted spoon and drain on kitchen paper. Serve with the sauce.

LENTIL DAL ★

This wonderful spicy sauce is so easy to make and a great way of adding protein and interest to a simple plate of vegetables or grains. I love it and make it often, sometimes varying it by adding a fried onion with the remaining spices, or topping it with a crunchy garnish of chopped garlic fried in 2–3 tablespoons of oil.

serves 4

250 g (9 oz) split red lentils
1 large onion, chopped
1 bay leaf
½ teaspoon turmeric powder
1 tablespoon fresh ginger, grated
2 teaspoons ground cumin
2 teaspoons ground coriander
3 garlic cloves, crushed
juice of 1 lemon

Put the lentils into a large saucepan with the onion, bay leaf, turmeric, ginger and 900 ml (1½ pints) water. Bring to the boil and simmer for 20 minutes, until the lentils are tender and pale. Remove and discard the bay leaf.

Put the cumin and coriander into a small saucepan and stir over the heat for a few seconds, until they smell aromatic and gorgeous, then stir them into the dal.

Add the garlic and lemon juice and season with salt and pepper to taste.

LEMONS Lemons must be one of the most useful flavourings; their fresh sharpness complements so many other ingredients, as well as being extremely appealing in its own right. Always use freshly squeezed lemon juice, both for its flavour and health-giving properties – it's a wonderful source of vitamin C, supports the immune system, has liver-cleansing properties – and lowers the GI of other foods.

MIDDLE EASTERN LENTILS AND SPINACH ★

Who would think that such cheap and simple foods could taste so good and be so deeply satisfying? This is such a comforting dish, too, and packed with iron and all kinds of other goodies. Serve on its own, or with a cooked grain for a perfectly balanced meal. Any leftovers are great cold.

serves 4

I tablespoon olive oil
I onion, sliced
I teaspoon ground coriander
I teaspoon ground cumin
500 g (I lb 2oz) spinach
2 × 425 g cans of Puy or green lentils, drained
2 garlic cloves, crushed
juice of ½ a lemon

Warm the olive oil in a large saucepan, add the onion and cook gently for about 7 minutes, or until tender.

Add the coriander and cumin and stir for a few seconds over the heat as the aroma is released, then cram in the spinach. Continue to cook for about 10 minutes, as the spinach shrinks and becomes tender. You could cut it a few times with the end of a fish slice and move it around a bit to help it to cook evenly.

When the spinach is done, add the lentils and cook gently for a few minutes until they're hot. Then stir in the garlic, lemon juice and salt and pepper to taste.

GARLIC Garlic as a flavouring needs no introduction, and its therapeutic properties are well documented. It's a potent natural anti-viral that, unlike the antibiotics you get from the doctor, only kills off bad bacteria, so you've still got the friendly ones that you need to keep you healthy. It also seems to help stop the spread of cancer. Over time, I've found myself using more and more of it, and chopping or slicing rather than crushing it. I've recently realized, however, that to get the full benefit of garlic's health-giving properties, you have got to use it raw or only barely heated. So recently I've gone back to crushing it (or, to be specific, grating it), then adding it to food at the end of cooking.

PUY LENTIL CASSEROLE ★

This is simple, warming and delicious, with a taste of the south of France about it.

serves 4

1 tablespoon olive oil
1 onion, peeled and chopped
500 g (1 lb 2 oz) leeks
500 g (1 lb 2 oz) carrots
2 bay leaves
2–3 sprigs of thyme or rosemary
250 g (9 oz) Puy lentils
425 g can of chopped tomatoes
3–4 garlic cloves, crushed
extra olive oil and chopped parsley (optional)

Warm the olive oil in a large saucepan, add the onion and cook gently, covered, for 7 minutes.

Meanwhile, wash and trim the leeks as necessary and cut into chunky pieces. Scrub or scrape the carrots and slice. Add these vegetables to the pan along with the bay leaves and thyme or rosemary, and leave to cook gently for a further 4–5 minutes.

Stir in the lentils and add 1 litre (1¾ pints) water, bring to the boil, then cover and leave to cook for about 30 minutes, or until the lentils and vegetables are tender.

Add the tomatoes, mix, and leave to cook for a further 10–15 minutes. Stir in the garlic and salt and pepper to taste just before serving.

Some good-quality olive oil drizzled over the top of this is excellent, as is a final garnish of chopped parsley – but it's also very good without.

CEREALS AND GRAINS

UNLIKE REFINED WHITE FLOUR AND PRODUCTS MADE FROM IT, MOST WHOLE GRAINS AND THEIR FLOURS, AS WELL AS PROVIDING A WIDE RANGE OF VITAMINS, MINERALS, PROTEIN AND FIBRE, HAVE A LOW GLYCAEMIC INDEX. THEY HAVE A VALUABLE – AND DELICIOUS – PART TO PLAY IN A HEALTHY, BALANCED VEGETARIAN DIET. USE THEM TO BRING VARIETY AND INTEREST AS WELL AS NOURISHMENT TO MEALS. EAT THEM JUDICIOUSLY, THOUGH, WHEN YOU ARE TRYING TO LOSE WEIGHT – THEN IT'S BETTER TO FILL UP WITH PULSES.

GRAINS

Barley
One of the reasons I love barley is that it's a grain which grows well in the UK, even in the colder north. It's also so modest and unassuming, yet nourishing and sweet-tasting. I like to use organic pearl barley, which, though 'polished', still has more fibre than brown rice. Barley flour is available from health food and organic shops and I love to use this for baking. I agree with Elizabeth David who said, 'Those who acquire a taste for it are likely to become addicts. I am one.' So am I.

Buckwheat
Buckwheat is such a lovely grain – or, technically, a seed – and, I think, greatly under-used. It's particularly good for the old and the young because it's very easy to digest (it's better in this respect than rice), and for women because it's a rich source of some of the nutrients that women tend to lack: magnesium, zinc, vitamin B6, iron, folic acid and calcium. It also contains rutin, which is helpful for high blood pressure and varicose veins. In this book you'll find recipes for using the grain and also for buckwheat noodles (see page 64).

Corn
Better known in the UK as sweetcorn and used as a vegetable, it is nutritious, has a low GI and can be eaten freely while losing weight. You can buy the dried kernels of popping corn to make your own popcorn for a low-GI snack that you can eat freely, especially if you have it with salt rather than sugary coatings.

Millet
Golden millet, which cooks to a fluffy consistency and, if you roast it as suggested, tastes delicately nutty, contains more protein and iron than most grains (though quinoa has the most protein), plus potassium, magnesium and phosphorous. It's also easier to digest than most grains, but has a higher GI than some, so best eaten with fruit or vegetables.

Oats
There's something sensual and soothing about the flavour and creamy consistency of oats. I use organic rolled oats for porridge and muesli mixes, oat bran and germ to stir into soya yoghurt for my current favourite breakfast, and medium or fine oatmeal for baking. All are delicious.

Quinoa
Confusingly pronounced 'keen-wa', quinoa is exceptional because weight for weight it contains more protein than meat and is a useful source of calcium. It's also got a very low GI rating, so will sustain you without sending your blood sugar racing. Along with millet and buckwheat, it makes an excellent healthy alternative to couscous. It's also available 'popped', to add to muesli.

Rice

All types of rice register on the high side on the glycaemic index; the lowest are brown and white basmati, which are medium. So go easy on rice while you want to lose weight, or avoid it altogether. Once you've reached your goal, or if weight is not an issue, try rice again in moderate portions, with vegetables and other ingredients with a low GI rating to bring down the total of the whole meal.

Wild rice

Technically a seed, though treated as a grain, wild rice has a delicious, smoky flavour, a chewy texture and a certain elegance. I love it mixed with rice.

COOKING GRAINS

It's often easier to measure grains by volume rather than weight: a 300 ml (½ pint) cup of cereals weighs approximately 225 g (8 oz). When cooked, grains roughly triple in weight and volume.

One cup of:	Cups of liquid	Cooking time	Notes
Barley, organic pearl	2–3	20–30 mins	Grains look plump and juicy and are tender when done.
Buckwheat, untoasted organic	2	15 mins	Wash then toast in pan as described on page 132. Add boiling water, cover and leave to stand for 15 mins, until grains are tender but still intact. Stir gently.
Millet	2	15 mins	Stir grains in a dry pan over heat for 3–4 mins, until they smell toasted, then pour in water and cook. Grains look pale and are tender when done. Leave to stand, covered, for 5 mins to 'fluff'.
Quinoa	2	15 mins	Grains look pearly with 'Saturn' ring when done. Leave to stand, covered, for 5 mins to 'fluff'.
Rice, brown organic	2–2½	40–45 mins	Grains are swollen and tender, with a slightly creamy texture when done. Leave to stand, still covered, for 10–15 mins, then stir gently with a fork.
Rice, brown basmati	2	30 mins	Grains are tender but separate and with some bite when done. Leave to stand, still covered, for 5–10 mins, then stir gently with a fork.
Rice, white basmati	1–1¼	14 mins	Cook over a very gentle heat, tightly covered. Leave to stand, undisturbed, for 8 mins, then stir gently with a fork.
Wild rice	4	45–50 mins	Grains split when tender, showing white insides.

GOLDEN RICE, AVOCADOS AND WILD MUSHROOMS

This consists of a protein-rich mixture of rice and split red lentils, served
with avocados, wild mushrooms and garlic. Everyone loves this
combination, though either part – the rice and lentils, or the stuffed
avocados – can be used separately.

serves 4

250 g (9 oz) basmati and wild rice mix
115 g (4 oz) split red lentils
¼ teaspoon turmeric
500 g (1 lb 2 oz) assorted wild mushrooms, cleaned
1 tablespoon olive oil
2 garlic cloves, chopped
juice of ½ a lemon, plus an extra squeeze
2 avocados

Preheat the oven to 150°C/300°F/Gas Mark 2.

Put the rice and lentils into a saucepan with the turmeric and 600 ml (1 pint) water. Bring to the boil,
then cover and leave to cook for 15 minutes. Remove from the heat and leave, still covered, for 5 minutes.

Fry the wild mushrooms in the oil in a large saucepan for 5–10 minutes, or until tender, adding the garlic
and a squeeze of lemon juice towards the end. Season with salt and pepper.

Halve, stone and peel the avocados, coat on both sides with lemon juice and salt and pepper. Add the
remaining lemon juice to the rice and lentil mixture – it will immediately brighten the colour.

Fluff the rice and lentils with a fork, adding a little salt, then spread on a serving plate. Top with the
avocado halves, cut-sides up. Spoon the mushrooms onto them, heaping them up but leaving a rim of
green showing. Put into a cool oven for up to 15 minutes while you eat your first course, but don't let
the avocados get too hot – warmed is fine, but not cooked or they'll spoil.

MOROCCAN CHICK PEA CASSEROLE

This is an easy, self-contained dish that's full of flavour. Just serve it with a leafy salad or a Middle Eastern Carrot Salad (page 70).

serves 4–6

- **2 onions, chopped**
- **2 tablespoons olive oil**
- **2 teaspoons cumin seeds**
- **2 teaspoons coriander seeds, lightly crushed**
- **4 garlic cloves, chopped**
- **2 aubergines, cut into chunky pieces**
- **1 red chilli**
- **4 g packet or 1 teaspoon saffron strands**
- **1 teaspoon salt**
- **2 × 425 g cans of chick peas**
- **175 g (6 oz) basmati white rice**
- **115 g (4 oz) large green olives**
- **1 thin-skinned lemon, sliced**
- **400 ml (¾ pint) vegetable stock**
- **handful of fresh coriander, roughly chopped**

Fry the onions in the oil in a large pan for 5 minutes. Stir in the cumin and coriander seeds, the garlic, aubergines, chilli, saffron and salt and leave to cook for a couple of minutes while you drain the chick peas into a sieve and rinse under the tap (to get rid of excess salt).

Add the chick peas to the pan along with the rice, olives and lemon slices, then pour in the stock. Bring to the boil, cover and cook gently for 20 minutes. Let it stand undisturbed for 5–10 minutes, then fork the chopped coriander through and serve.

BREAKFAST RECIPES

IRON-RICH BREAKFAST MIX

I owe this (and indeed some of the iron-boosting ideas on page 23) to Peter Cox and his *Encyclopaedia of Vegetarian Living*. Mix together 25 g (1 oz) each of sesame seeds and sunflower seeds, and 50 g (2 oz) each of pistachios, pumpkin seeds and rolled oats. Stir in 1 tablespoon of blackstrap molasses and enough fruit juice to cover and leave to soak. Serve with fresh fruit to taste. This provides a hefty 25 mg of iron; you could eat it in two or more portions throughout the day.

FRUIT SMOOTHIES

A fruit smoothie makes a nourishing breakfast, or snack at any time, and is very easy to make if you have a food processor, blender or a stick blender. All you do is whiz together chopped fruit and liquid until smooth and creamy. You can freeze the chunks of fruit or use ready-frozen fruit for a luscious thick and icy drink: chunks of frozen peeled banana are especially good for this, whizzed with apple, orange or pineapple juice, soya milk or plain yogurt. Blueberries, raspberries, strawberries and ripe peaches are great, too, and you can add flavourings such as vanilla or cinnamon, and a tablespoon of ground almonds or flax seeds for extra nutrients and thickness if you wish.

MUESLI OR GRANOLA

There are many muesli and granola mixes on the market, and which one you choose – or whether you make your own – is really a question of taste. I'd go for an organic mix, without added sugar, although some good ones have a little sweetening from apple juice and a touch of honey. A luxurious organic version contains jumbo oats, crunchy oat bran flakes, roasted hazelnuts, pumpkin seeds, sesame seeds and dried fruit: blueberries, cranberries, nectarines and strawberries. You could make something similar by combining these ingredients yourself. Toast the grains, nuts and seeds lightly in a moderate oven for 15–20 minutes, if you like, stirring them a few times. Cool, then mix with the dried fruit. You could also add a little 'popped' quinoa (see page 114), from health-food shops, for wonderful balanced protein, and, just before serving, sprinkle on a tablespoon of freshly ground golden flax seeds for omega-3 oils.

TOFU SCRAMBLE

Mash the drained contents of a 250 g packet of firm or silken tofu until it looks like scrambled eggs. Heat 1 tablespoon of olive oil in a saucepan, add the mashed tofu, half a teaspoon of turmeric for colour, 1 tablespoon of soy sauce, some salt and freshly ground black pepper, and stir until hot, then serve as it is, or on hot toast. You could fry a chopped onion, garlic, tomatoes or sliced mushrooms in the oil before adding the tofu, for extra interest.

PORRIDGE

Measure 1 cup of rolled oats or another grain, such as flaked rice, barley or quinoa (or a mixture of these) into a saucepan and add 1 cup of water and 1 cup of milk or soya milk. Stir over the heat for a few minutes until thick and creamy. Serve as it is or topped with flaked almonds, raisins, soaked dried fruit, chopped fresh fruit, a swirl of apple juice concentrate, a few flaked almonds, a scattering of ground flax seeds, some sesame seeds or gomashio (see page 158).

SOYA YOGURT

There is a wonderful thick and creamy unsweetened soya yogurt that I first discovered in France and which now, I'm thrilled to say, is available from good health-food shops and organic outlets. I love to eat it chilled, straight from the pot. You might also try it swirled with maple syrup, with chopped dried, fresh or soaked fruit, or with toasted nuts and seeds. If you want to make your own soya yogurt, use an electric yogurt maker, following the maker's instructions, using a little live cow's or goat's milk yogurt to start it off, then saving a bit of soya yogurt from each batch to start the next. Alternatively do as I do – sterilize three 450 g (1 lb) jam jars by heating them in a cool oven for 10 minutes or so. Cool, then put 1 teaspoon of live yogurt into each and top up with soya milk that feels comfortably hot to your finger. Screw on the lids, wrap in a warm towel or blanket and put in an airing cupboard or by a radiator for about 8 hours until set.

VEGETARIAN SUSHI

Once you get into the swing of it, these are much quicker to roll up than you'd think. If you're making them for a party, it's best to include the wasabi – hot Japanese mustard – in the rolls, along with a little pickled ginger and a drizzle of dipping sauce, but if you're doing them for a small number of people, it's more fun for everyone to have their own little dollop of wasabi, a small pile of pink pickled ginger furls and a tiny bowl of dipping sauce. You can buy all these things, and mirin, at an Oriental food shop. While you're there, buy one of the small woven mats they sell for rolling the sushi on – but don't worry if you haven't got one, just improvise with a square of polythene. The vinegar, the seaweed and the coldness all lower the GI of the sushi rice: using basmati rice instead would lower it even more.

makes 40–48

250 g (9 oz) Japanese
   sticky rice
2 tablespoons rice vinegar
2 tablespoons mirin
I teaspoon salt
5–6 sheets of nori
   seaweed, ready toasted

FOR THE FILLING
I red pepper, grilled,
   cooled and skinned
I golden pepper, grilled,
   cooled and skinned
I small avocado
4–6 asparagus spears,
   not too fat
small piece of plain or
   smoky tofu

FOR THE DIP
3 tablespoons soy sauce
3 tablespoons mirin
I teaspoon grated fresh
   ginger
½ teaspoon sesame seeds

TO SERVE
wasabi
Japanese pickled ginger

Put the rice into a saucepan with 600 ml (I pint) water. Bring to the boil, then cover, turn the heat down and leave to cook very gently for 15 minutes. Stir in the vinegar, mirin and salt. Cover the pan and leave to cool.

Next, prepare the fillings. You need long strips, about the size of the asparagus spears, so cut your peppers, avocado and tofu accordingly. You'll only need a few strips of each.

Now for the fun. Put your sushi mat or a piece of polythene about 22 × 24 cm (8½ × 9½ in) in front of you. Have a little bowl of cold water by you for dipping your fingers, and your rice and ingredients to hand.

Put a sheet of nori on the mat and spoon about 3 tablespoons of sticky rice on top. Using your fingers, spread it over the nori, leaving 1 cm (½ in) clear all round. Don't worry if there are some gaps. Take one of your fillings – the asparagus spears are easy to start with – and lay them on top of the rice along the end nearest to you, about 1 cm (½ in) in from the edge of the rice.

Then, starting with the end nearest to you, pull the edge of the nori and the rice up against the asparagus spears and then keep rolling it, firmly, like a Swiss roll, using the mat or polythene to help you. When it's done, give it one more press to hold it all together and put it onto a plate.

Continue like this using the other fillings, on their own or a couple at a time, until you've used all the rice and have 5 or 6 rolls. Chill them for at least 30 minutes, then, using a sharp serrated knife, cut each roll into about 8 pieces, discarding the ends.

To make the dipping sauce, just mix everything together and put into a small bowl or bowls. Serve the sushi with the dipping sauce, wasabi and pickled ginger.

SUSHI HANDROLLS Serve small squares of nori and all the ingredients in little bowls and let people roll their own nori into cone shapes and fill them with sushi rice and their chosen fillings. Serve with the wasabi, pickled ginger, dipping sauce and sesame seeds.

SEAWEEDS, SEA VEGETABLES Like many of the more unusual ingredients in this book, seaweed is something that really grows on you! It contains numerous nutrients (see page 13); some seaweeds even contain the elusive long-chain omega-3 fatty acids. Flavourwise, I think seaweed is exquisite. Buy some, try it and see. Flat sheets of toasted nori are easy to use – just snip shreds over the top of steamed or stir-fried vegetables, salads or grain dishes, or make them into sushi rolls or cones (see above). Hijiki and arame are particular favourites of mine. Both need rinsing, then simmering in a little water for a few minutes until they're tender. Don't let the potent smell of the sea that arises put you off; once they're cooked, they don't taste or smell strong. You'll find recipes using them on pages 158 and 160; I wish there had been room for more. I didn't have space, either, for recipes using wakame or dulse, but you prepare and use them in the same way, and they're equally delicious. Kombu is useful because it helps to tenderize beans and gives flavour to grains – just rinse a piece to remove excess salt, and add it to the pot. Remove after cooking and discard, though some addicts have been known to cut it up and eat it, maybe sprinkled with a little rice vinegar and soy sauce.

RISOTTO WITH ROSEMARY AND LEMON

This simple risotto needs very few ingredients yet tastes divine. You can even make a particularly delicious vegan version (see below). For GI 'correctness', serve in small to moderate portions with a cooked vegetable such as French beans or a green salad.

serves 6

1 tablespoon olive oil
1 celery heart, finely chopped
1 bunch of salad onions, chopped
2 large garlic cloves, crushed
400 g (14 oz) Arborio or risotto rice
2 glasses of vermouth or white wine
1.2 litres (2 pints) vegetable stock
grated zest of 1 lemon
1 tablespoon rosemary, chopped
50 g (2 oz) butter
115 g (4 oz) Parmesan cheese, grated

Heat the olive oil in a large saucepan, add the celery and salad onions. Stir, then add the garlic and rice. Stir again, then pour in the vermouth or wine and let it bubble away as you stir.

Now add a ladleful of the stock, still stirring. When it has been absorbed, add another ladleful and continue until the rice is tender – about 25 minutes. Stir in the grated lemon zest, rosemary, butter and Parmesan. Cover with a folded cloth and leave for a minute or two for them to melt creamily into the rice, then stir with a fork and serve.

I like this with a leafy salad containing some peppery leaves like rocket or watercress.

For a vegan version, leave out the Parmesan and butter and instead stir in another couple of tablespoons of olive oil and 120 ml of soya cream (see page 169) into the risotto for a very silky, yummy dish.

WARM BEETROOT AND QUINOA TABBOULEH ★

I love raw grated beetroot and one day I served it with some hot cooked quinoa. They mixed together on my plate and that was enough to set me off. Several versions later, this one, with the sweetness of the onion, is everyone's favourite, though for a simpler version you could leave the onion out and serve it as it is, or maybe with a few raisins stirred in.

serves 4

115 g (4 oz) quinoa
2 tablespoons olive oil
2 large red onions, finely sliced
2 tablespoons balsamic vinegar
2 tablespoons freshly squeezed lemon juice
2 small raw beetroots, grated (about 200 g/7 oz)
handful of flat-leaf parsley, coarsely chopped, plus extra to serve
red chard leaves or other green salad leaves, to serve

Put the quinoa in a sieve and rinse thoroughly under the cold tap, then put into a saucepan with 300 ml (½ pint) water and bring to the boil. Cover and leave to cook slowly for 15 minutes. Remove from the heat and leave to stand, still covered, for 5 minutes.

Meanwhile, warm the olive oil in a roomy saucepan, add the onions, stir to coat with the oil, then cover and leave to cook gently for 10 minutes, or until very tender.

Stir the balsamic vinegar into the onions, let it bubble, then remove from the heat and add the quinoa, lemon juice, beetroot, parsley and plenty of salt and freshly ground black pepper to taste. Scatter over a little more parsley and serve with red chard leaves.

CEREALS AND GRAINS

MILLET WITH PEPPERY LEAVES AND AVOCADO

'Peppery leaves' can include watercress and wild rocket, along with some reddish baby lettuce leaves.

serves 4 as a side dish or starter, 2 as a main course

> **125 g (4 oz) millet**
> **a few pine nuts**
> **1 ripe avocado**
> **85g (3 oz) rocket, watercress and other leaves**
> **grated zest and juice of 1 lemon or lime**
> **1–2 tablespoons olive oil**

Put the millet into a sieve and rinse under the cold tap, then tip into a saucepan and stir over a moderate heat for 3–4 minutes until the millet has dried and is beginning to smell toasted.

Pour 300 ml (½ pint) or 1 cup boiling water into the millet. Be prepared for the mixture to seethe and steam as the water is added – the steam can be very hot so protect your hand if necessary. Add a pinch of salt, cover the pan and leave to cook gently for 15 minutes.

Remove the pan from the heat and leave to stand for 5 minutes – the millet will become dry and fluffy.

Meanwhile, toast the pine nuts. Spread them out on a dry baking sheet and put under a hot grill for a minute or so. As soon as they turn golden (watch them carefully), remove them from the grill and tip into a cold dish so they don't go on cooking and burn.

Peel and slice the avocado. Put the salad leaves around the sides of a bowl or serving dish. Spoon the millet into the centre and scatter the avocado over the top. Drizzle the lemon or lime juice and olive oil over, sprinkle with salt, the lemon or lime zest and the toasted pine nuts, grind over some pepper and serve.

MILLET AND CAULIFLOWER MASH

When you purée cooked millet and cauliflower together they look like mashed potatoes, and are a favourite in macrobiotic diets in which potatoes are generally avoided. I like this mixture because it's a different way of serving a grain and has a lower GI rating than mashed potatoes. It goes with anything that's good with mashed potatoes, such as the Grilled Seitan with Onions (page 154), or any bean dish. If there's any left over, form it into little 'cakes', coat with flour and fry in olive oil until crisp and golden, for potato-style cakes.

serves 4–6

225 g (8 oz) millet
1 medium cauliflower (about 450 g/1 lb after trimming)
2 tablespoons olive oil
2 garlic cloves, crushed
1 tablespoon Dijon mustard
4–6 tablespoons parsley, chopped
2 salad onions, chopped

Put the millet into a dry pan and set over a medium heat for about 4 minutes, stirring often, until it smells toasted and gorgeous. Standing back, because it will sizzle, pour in 600 ml (1 pint) water, cover and leave to cook for 15 minutes. It will be pale, fluffy and all the water will have been absorbed.

Meanwhile, divide the cauliflower into florets and cook in 2.5 cm (1 in) boiling water in a pan, covered, until tender. This should take about 6–7 minutes, depending on the size of the pieces. Drain, saving the water.

Purée the cauliflower and millet in a food processor, adding a little of the cauliflower water, if necessary, to make a creamy mixture, then add the olive oil, garlic, mustard, parsley, salad onions and some salt and pepper to taste, and whiz again briefly.

OATCAKES

Why bother to make oatcakes? Because these are unlike any you can buy: thin, crisp and, I think, utterly delicious. But you must use the right oatmeal – very fine, almost like flour. Eat them with soft goat's cheese or any of the dips on pages 88 and 89. I particularly like them with the Light and Creamy Hummus. Or serve them for breakfast with butter and honey for a real treat.

makes 16

140 g (5 oz) fine oatmeal, plus extra for rolling out
½ teaspoon salt
1 teaspoon olive oil

Preheat the oven to 180°C/350°F/Gas Mark 4.

Put the oatmeal into a bowl. Mix the salt and olive oil with 125 ml (4 fl oz) boiling water, stir to dissolve the salt, then pour over the oatmeal and mix. Leave for a few minutes to allow the oatmeal to swell, then divide the mixture in half and form each into a ball.

Roll out each ball of dough to a circle, using plenty of oatmeal on your board to prevent sticking, then cut into 8 equal slices, like a cake.

Take each slice and roll it from edge to edge, making it as thin as you can. Place on a baking sheet – they can be close together as they won't spread – and bake for 10 minutes, until the top is set, then turn them over and bake for a further 5 minutes, to cook the other side.

Cool on a wire rack, then serve. Store any left over in an airtight tin.

BUCKWHEAT WITH LEMON AND HERBS

Buckwheat is almost as quick to prepare as couscous and bulgar wheat but much better for you and far more interesting. Prepared simply, as here, it makes a superb accompaniment to all kinds of vegetable dishes – roasted, stir-fried, etc – or it can be turned into the focus of a meal by adding some more substantial ingredients, such as cubes of feta cheese, marinated tofu or cashew nuts. I recommend organic untoasted buckwheat – it's far nicer than the other types.

serves 4

250 g (9 oz) organic, untoasted buckwheat
1 tablespoon olive oil
long strands of zest from 1 lemon
juice of 1 lemon
4 heaped tablespoons flat-leaf parsley, chopped
4 heaped tablespoons chives, chopped
6 salad onions, cut into shreds

Rinse the buckwheat in a sieve under the cold tap, then put it into a dry saucepan and cook over a moderate heat for about 5 minutes, stirring it about from time to time, until it smells gorgeously toasty and looks a bit more golden.

Pour 600 ml (1 pint) boiling water into the saucepan, standing well back. Then cover the pan and leave for 15 minutes, off the heat for an al dente result (which I prefer) or over a gentle heat if you want it softer. I told you it was as easy as couscous!

Using a fork, stir the olive oil, lemon zest and juice, parsley, chives and salad onions into the buckwheat. Season with salt and pepper and serve.

SAFFRON RISOTTO CAKE WITH RED PEPPERS

This can be made in advance and kept in the fridge or freezer ready for cooking.

serves 6–8

butter or margarine, for greasing
2 tablespoons dried breadcrumbs
2 red peppers, seeded and halved
2 tablespoons olive oil
I onion, peeled and chopped
2 large garlic cloves, crushed
400 g (14 oz) Arborio or risotto rice
4 g packet or I teaspoon saffron threads
150 ml (¼ pint) vermouth or white wine
I teaspoon vegetable bouillon powder
115 g (4 oz) freshly grated Parmesan cheese (optional)
some red pepper strips and green leaves, eg flat-leaf parsley, to serve

Preheat the oven to 180°C/350°F/Gas Mark 4. Line the base of a 900 g (2 lb) loaf tin with a strip of non-stick paper, then grease with butter or margarine and sprinkle with breadcrumbs.

Grill the peppers, cut-side down, for about 10 minutes, or until tender and black in places. Leave to cool.

Heat the olive oil in a large saucepan and add the onion. Stir, then cover and cook for 7 minutes. Add the garlic, rice and saffron. Stir well, then pour in the vermouth or wine and let it bubble away as you stir.

Measure 850 ml (1½ pints) of boiling water into a pan, add the bouillon powder and keep the water very gently simmering. Add a ladleful to the rice, stirring. When this has been absorbed, add another ladleful and continue until all the liquid has been added and the rice is tender – about 25 minutes. Stir in the Parmesan, if using. Cover the pan with a cloth. Leave for 5 minutes to settle, then season.

Remove the skins from the peppers – you don't need to be too particular about this; just get off the black bits that will come away easily. Put a third of the rice mixture into the loaf tin, then place two pepper halves on top. Spoon another third of the rice on top, followed by two more pepper halves, then the rest of the rice. Press down well.

Cover the tin with foil and bake for 30–40 minutes. Remove from the oven and let it stand for 3–4 minutes, then slip a knife round the sides and turn it out onto a warm serving dish. Garnish with pieces of red pepper and green leaves.

To serve, cut into thick slices with a sharp knife. It needs to be treated gently when warm.

BARLEY AND MUSHROOM RISOTTO

Barley is a gorgeous, plump, sweet grain that needn't be confined to stews and soups; it can be quite glamorous if you make it into a risotto. I love to use juicy chestnut mushrooms and, to start the risotto off, whisky seems the natural thing to use (cook's whisky, of course, nothing fancy).

serves 4

15 g packet or 1 tablespoon dried porcini mushrooms
2 teaspoons vegetable bouillon powder
1 onion, finely chopped
2 sticks celery, finely chopped
2 tablespoons olive oil
4 garlic cloves, chopped
500 g (1 lb 2 oz) chestnut mushrooms, sliced
350 g (12 oz) organic pearl barley
100 ml (3½ fl oz) whisky
25–50 g (1–2 oz) butter (optional)
Parmesan cheese flakes, to serve (optional)

Put the dried porcini into a saucepan with 1.2 litres (2 pints) water and the bouillon powder. Bring to the boil, then set aside.

Fry the onion and celery in the oil for 5 minutes, then add the garlic, mushrooms and barley and stir so that they become glossy with oil.

Pour in the whisky and when it has sizzled away, stir in a ladleful of the porcini water. Keep stirring, and when the liquid has boiled away again, add another ladleful. Continue in this way until all the water, and the porcini mushrooms in it, have been added and the barley is soft and creamy. This will take about 30–35 minutes and you can be more relaxed about the stirring as the cooking goes on.

Take the pan off the heat, stir in the butter, if using, and season to taste. Then leave the pan, covered, to stand for 10 minutes. Serve with Parmesan flakes, if using.

LEMONY RICE

This pretty, primrose yellow rice is easy to do and goes with many spicy dishes. The lemon gives it a fresh flavour, brightens up the colour and lowers the GI rating.

serves 4 as an accompaniment

1 teaspoon turmeric
250 g (9 oz) basmati rice
grated zest and juice of 1 lemon

Bring 1 litre (1¾ pints) water to the boil in a saucepan, stir in the turmeric and add the rice. Boil, uncovered, for 6–7 minutes, or until a grain is tender but still has a little resistance.

Drain the rice into a sieve, then put it back into the saucepan with salt and pepper to taste.

Using a fork, gently stir in the lemon zest and juice. As you do so, the rice will change from a dull gold to an uplifting, bright, primrose yellow. Reheat gently and serve.

LEMONY RICE WITH WILD RICE Instead of plain white basmati rice, buy a packet of basmati and wild rice mixed, and use that instead – the dark strands of wild rice look pretty against the golden rice, and taste good, too.

NATURAL PROTEIN FOODS

TOFU, TEMPEH AND SEITAN ARE THE ORIGINAL VEGETARIAN PROTEIN FOODS, AND HAVE BEEN USED IN CHINA AND JAPAN FOR CENTURIES. THEY'RE MADE FROM NATURAL INGREDIENTS – SOYA, IN THE CASE OF TOFU AND TEMPEH; WHEAT GLUTEN FOR SEITAN – AND IF, LIKE ME, YOU BUY THEM IN THEIR SIMPLE, TRADITIONAL FORM (AS OPPOSED TO 'BACON FLAVOURED', ETC), THEY MAKE A WONDERFUL BASE FOR ALL KINDS OF MEALS. THEY'RE ALL RICH IN PROTEIN AND LOW IN FAT AND CARBOHYDRATES, AND ARE VERY HEALTH-GIVING, AS WELL AS BEING EASY TO USE AND DELICIOUS.

NATURAL PROTEIN FOODS

Tofu

This is made by first soaking, then puréeing, gently simmering and straining soya beans to make soya milk. This is mixed with an acidic ingredient such as calcium chloride, which separates it into curds and whey. The curds are strained into a mould and pressed, and the result is tofu. It's a natural process that you could undertake at home, and indeed I have. These days, however, I prefer to buy it from the chiller cabinet of a good health shop. The various brands have slightly different tastes and textures so experiment with a few to find the one you prefer. You can buy both firm and silken tofu. I use firm for everything, but silken is good for creamy dips, dressings and fools. You also can get various 'flavoured' tofus and products based on it, but it's just as easy to add your own flavourings.

Tempeh

Tempeh (pronounced 'tem-pay') is made from cooked soya beans that have been fermented. It's been made like in this in Indonesia for centuries and is a traditional food throughout the country. It's very digestible, so is a useful high-protein, low-fat nutritious food for the very young and the elderly. It looks like a café-au-lait-coloured slab with a lumpy texture, and is to be found in the chiller cabinets of the same specialist health shops that sell good-quality tofu. Choose a pale one without black flecks in it: the flecks are part of the fermentation process and are edible but tend to give the tempeh a stronger flavour. The simplest way to prepare tempeh is to slice it, brush with a little olive oil and grill it, then sprinkle with soy sauce or spread with a spicy chutney.

Seitan

Seitan (pronounced 'say-tan') is another protein ingredient that's so natural and traditional you could easily make it at home. You make a dough from strong plain flour and water, knead it, soak it then rinse it, pressing and rinsing until a white liquid comes out: this is the starch. When the water runs clear and the 'dough' becomes bouncy and springy, that's your seitan. Alternatively you can mix gluten powder (from www.flourbin.com) to a dough with water. Either way, you then simmer it in flavoured stock, drain and use as required.

You can buy seitan in the same places that sell good tofu and tempeh, either in the chiller cabinet, or in a jar, marinated in tamari. It's very high in protein and virtually fat-free.

To cook seitan, drain it, pat dry and slice with a sharp knife – I like it cut quite thin. Then either toss in a little olive oil and grill, or shallow-fry, until crisp.

WARM SMOKY TOFU AND BROCCOLI SALAD ★

I love this combination of crisp, smoky tofu and tender broccoli, with its
sweet and sour gingery dressing. And it's so quick and easy to make.

serves 2 for a main meal

> **450 g (1 lb) broccoli**
> **250 g (9 oz) smoked tofu**
> **vegetable oil**
> **1 tablespoon soy sauce**
> **1 tablespoon toasted sesame oil**
> **1 tablespoon mirin**
> **1 tablespoon rice vinegar**
> **1 teaspoon grated ginger**
> **1 garlic clove, crushed**

Divide the broccoli into florets, cutting larger ones in half so they're all roughly the same size. In a
saucepan, bring 2.5 cm (1 in) of water to the boil. Add the broccoli, cover and cook for about 4 minutes,
until the broccoli is just tender to the point of a knife.

Meanwhile drain the tofu, pat dry on kitchen paper and cut into very thin slices. Pour about 3 tablespoons
of oil into a frying pan, heat and add a single layer of tofu. Fry until the tofu is crisp and brown on one
side, then flip the pieces over. When they're done, drain on kitchen paper. You will probably have to cook
the tofu in several batches.

Drain the broccoli, then put it back in the pan with the soy sauce, sesame oil, mirin, rice vinegar, grated
ginger and garlic. Toss lightly, then stir in the crisp tofu and serve.

VINEGARS I find the most useful are: rice vinegar, for Oriental dishes, and because it's so (naturally)
sweet and light that you can use more than the usual proportions in dressings and so need less oil;
balsamic vinegar – as good a one as I can afford – for its sweetness; red wine vinegar, although I find I use
this a lot less than I used to because I'm so fond of rice vinegar, and also because I've gone back to my
vegetarian roots and taken to using organic apple cider vinegar again. The latter is light, sweet and fruity,
and is also said to alkalize the system and have all kinds of therapeutic properties, including staving off or
easing arthritis.

GRIDDLED TOFU WITH CHILLI, PAK CHOY AND GINGER ★

Tofu can taste superb – yes, it really can. It all starts, as with most cookery, with your choice of ingredients. Buy the right type of tofu (see page 140), cook it with lively flavourings and you've got a dish anyone would enjoy. Using a griddle pan gives the tofu attractive stripes, but if you haven't got one, cut the tofu into cubes and cook with the mushrooms instead. It will taste just as good.

serves 2

250 g block of organic, firm tofu
2 large garlic cloves, crushed
1 tablespoon grated fresh ginger
1–2 tablespoons soy sauce, plus a little extra for serving
1 tablespoon mirin
2 × 200 g packets of pak choy
2 tablespoons olive oil
250 g (9 oz) fresh shiitake or chestnut mushrooms, washed and sliced
½ a mild red chilli, seeded and chopped
2 small salad onions, sliced
1–2 teaspoons dark sesame oil (optional)
½–1 teaspoon toasted sesame seeds (see page 64)

Drain the tofu, then cut it across so that you have rectangles about 5 mm (¼ in) thick. Cut these into triangles and put into a shallow dish. Mix together half the garlic, half the ginger, the soy sauce and mirin and pour over the tofu, making sure all the pieces are coated. Set aside.

Wash and slice the pak choy. Heat 1 tablespoon of the oil in a wok or large saucepan and add the mushrooms, pak choy, chilli, salad onions and the remaining garlic and ginger. Stir-fry for about 6 minutes, or until the pak choy is tender but still crisp.

Meanwhile, brush the griddle pan with the remaining oil and heat. Pick up a piece of tofu, letting the excess liquid run back onto the plate. Put the tofu onto the hot griddle pan, then repeat with the rest of the tofu (you may have to do it in more than one batch, depending on the size of your griddle). Cook for 2–3 minutes, until the tofu is sealed and seared with appetizing brown stripes, then flip the pieces over to do the other side.

Add any remaining tofu marinade to the pak choy mixture, stir and season with salt, freshly ground black pepper, the sesame oil, if you're using it, and a dash of soy sauce. Serve with the griddled tofu, sprinkled with the sesame seeds.

TOFU AND MUSHROOM SKEWERS ★

Use two metal skewers, or two wooden ones that have been soaked in cold water for 10 minutes or more so that they won't burn in the heat. Serve with a herby Raita (page 71) and some Cumin-roasted Sweet Potatoes (page 46) if you're not slimming.

serves 2

250 g (9 oz) tofu
1 tablespoon soy sauce
1 tablespoon olive oil
1 tablespoon mirin
1 teaspoon grated ginger
1 garlic clove, crushed
85 g (3 oz) baby chestnut mushrooms

Drain the tofu, pat dry on kitchen paper and cut into cubes – about 10 is ideal. In a shallow dish that will hold the tofu, mix the soy sauce, olive oil, mirin, ginger and garlic to make a marinade. Add the tofu and turn it around so that it gets coated.

Wash the mushrooms but don't remove the stalks. Cut them in half, if necessary. Thread a mushroom onto a skewer followed by a cube of tofu, then another mushroom and so on – pack them well together. When both skewers are crammed full, brush them with the remaining soy sauce mixture. They can wait, sitting in their marinade, for some hours, or you can grill them straight away.

When you're ready, prepare a hot grill or barbecue. Put the skewers on a tray under the grill or on the barbecue and spoon any extra marinade over them. Cook until they're stickily brown and lightly caramelized and smell gorgeous – about 6 minutes under a hot grill, turning them after about 4 minutes. Serve at once.

FOR MARINATED TOFU Drain a 250 g (9 oz) block of tofu, pat dry with kitchen paper then slice or dice. In a shallow dish mix together 1 large crushed garlic clove, a good teaspoon of fresh grated ginger, 1–2 tablespoons of soy sauce and a tablespoon of apple juice concentrate or clear honey. Add the tofu, stir gently, and leave for at least 10 minutes, though several hours is better, stirring the pieces occasionally. You can eat it as it is, grill, barbecue or bake it, or add it to stir-fries.

SAUCES

TARTARE SAUCE

Pour 5 tablespoons of soya milk into a blender or food processor with 2 tablespoons of fresh lemon juice, I teaspoon of Dijon mustard, I tablespoon of wine vinegar or cider vinegar, a crushed small garlic clove, salt and pepper, and blend briefly. Drizzle 200 ml (7 fl oz) of light olive oil through the lid while continuing to process. It will become thick, like mayonnaise. Transfer to a bowl and serve as it is, or stir in I tablespoon of chopped capers and I tablespoon of chopped gherkins.

QUICK TOMATO SAUCE

A quick and easy sauce you can make all year round. Fry a chopped onion in I tablespoon of oil in a covered pan for 10 minutes. Stir in a chopped or crushed garlic clove and the contents of I x 425 g can tomatoes, or 500 g (1 lb 2 oz) fresh tomatoes, quartered, with or without their skins. Cook without a lid for 15 minutes. Whiz or blend it if you want it smooth, and pour it through a sieve if you kept the tomato skins on and want it smooth. Season with salt and pepper. Pour it over cooked vegetables such as leeks, broccoli or cauliflower for a main dish, maybe adding some drained canned pulses, slivers of fried tofu or a topping of grated cheese; serve it over pasta, pulses or cooked grains.

MADEIRA GRAVY

Heat 2 tablespoons of rapeseed oil in a saucepan. Add 2 tablespoons of fine wholemeal flour and stir over the heat for a minute or two until nut-brown. Then add a 15 g packet or I tablespoon of dried porcini mushrooms and 600 ml (1 pint) water or vegetable stock. Stir over the heat for 2–3 minutes, until thickened, then leave over a gentle heat for 7–10 minutes to cook the flour. Stir in I tablespoon of soy sauce, 2 tablespoons of madeira (or sherry) and salt and pepper to taste. Strain before using (reserving the pieces of porcini to use in future cooking), then whiz in a food processor until smooth. Alternatively do as I do and serve the gravy with the porcini still in it.

TAHINI OR PEANUT OR SOYA NUT SAUCE

Put 3 tablespoons of light tahini, peanut or soya-nut butter into a bowl and stir in 2 tablespoons of water and a crushed garlic clove. For the tahini sauce, stir in 1 tablespoon of freshly squeezed lemon juice; for the peanut or soya-nut sauce, add 1 teaspoon of honey or apple juice concentrate and 1 teaspoon of grated fresh ginger. Stir the sauces well. In each case, if you want the sauce thinner, stir in a little extra water.

CRANBERRY SAUCE

Wash 250 g (9 oz) cranberries, removing any damaged ones. Put the cranberries into a saucepan with 2 tablespoons of apple juice concentrate and 175 g (6 oz) caster sugar and place over a medium heat. Cook gently for 4–5 minutes, until the juices run and the cranberries soften but don't go mushy. Serve warm or cold. Alternatively, try this quick version, more like a relish: simply purée the raw cranberries to a chunky consistency with 4 tablespoons of honey, adding more to taste if necessary. This keeps for a week in the fridge.

LIGHT AND CREAMY WHITE SAUCE

Bring just under 600 ml (1 pint) soya milk to the boil in a saucepan with a bay leaf and a piece of onion. Leave to stand off the heat while you mix 2 tablespoons of cornflour with a little more soya milk in a bowl to make a smooth paste. Then reheat the milk, mix it into the paste and return it all to the pan. Stir over the heat for a minute or two until thickened. If you like, stir in a tablespoon or two of olive oil for extra richness (or a knob of butter, if you prefer), and salt, pepper and grated nutmeg to taste. Remove the onion and bay leaf before serving. You could also add freshly chopped parsley, grated cheese, or a tablespoon or so of nutritional yeast flakes for a 'cheesy' flavour. Soya milk tastes very creamy, but for an even richer version use 350 ml (12 fl oz) soya milk and a 250 ml carton of soya cream.

GRILLED SPICED TOFU WITH PEPPERS ★

So you think tofu is bland and has no flavour? Well, try this. Sambal Oelek
is an Indonesian hot pepper sauce that you can get at any supermarket
(read the label and check you're getting a vegetarian one). It keeps for
ages in the fridge. The light coating of cornflour or gram flour makes the
tofu crisp. Serve with basmati rice and a leafy salad, if you like.

serves 2

1 red pepper, seeded and cut into long slices
250 g (9 oz) tofu
4–6 teaspoons Sambal Oelek
4–6 teaspoons gram flour (see page 106) or cornflour
olive oil
parsley, to garnish

Heat the grill to high. Start with the peppers, because these take longer to cook. Simply put them in a
grill pan and place under the grill.

Meanwhile, drain the tofu, cut in half horizontally, then halve each piece. Spread Sambal Oelek all over
the cut surfaces of the tofu, then toss the pieces in the gram flour or cornflour, pressing it in lightly.

Remove the grill pan from the grill, lightly oil the area where the tofu will go, then put the tofu on the
grill pan and turn immediately so the top of each piece is oily. Turn the pieces of pepper as necessary,
then put everything back under the grill.

Grill until the tofu is browned on top – maybe 4 minutes – then turn the pieces over. The other side
won't take as long and by then the peppers will be done, too. Serve at once, garnished with the parsley.

As a variation you could shallow-fry the tofu in oil.

QUICK TOFU CURRY WITH PEAS ★

Quick, easy, full of flavour and nourishment – what more could you ask of a dish? It's pretty good just on its own, but you could serve it with some plain boiled basmati rice (white or brown) or some nan bread. My favourite accompaniment is cauliflower or shredded cabbage, cooked until it's just tender.

serves 4

1 onion, chopped
2 tablespoons vegetable oil
2 garlic cloves, chopped
2 teaspoons grated fresh ginger
1 teaspoon cumin seeds
½ teaspoon turmeric
250 g (9 oz) tofu
3 tomatoes, roughly chopped
115 g (4 oz) frozen peas
1 tablespoon fresh lemon juice
a little fresh coriander (optional)

Cook the onion in the oil in a covered pan for 5 minutes, until the onion is beginning to soften. Stir in the garlic, ginger, cumin and turmeric and leave to cook for a minute or so.

Meanwhile, deal with the tofu: it needs to be drained, patted dry with kitchen paper and then cut into cubes. Add the tofu to the spicy mixture in the pan and cook for 5 minutes over a moderate heat, so that it becomes golden brown in places, stirring often.

Add the tomatoes and peas. Cook for 3–4 minutes, until the peas have heated through and the tomatoes have softened. Stir in the lemon juice, taste and season with salt and pepper. Snip some coriander over the top, if using, and serve.

TEMPEH BURGERS

Apart from just cutting it thinly, frying it till crisp and serving it with a salad or richly flavoured Madeira Gravy (page 146), this is my favourite way of using tempeh. This recipe makes four burgers, enough for two people, but the recipe is easily doubled to make enough for four people. I love these burgers with either a sweet sauce, like Cranberry Sauce (page 147), or with a sharp, creamy Tartare Sauce (page 146).

serves 2

200 g packet of tempeh
2 tablespoons vegetable oil
I onion, finely chopped
15 g (½ oz) cornflour
I garlic clove, crushed
100 ml (3½ fl oz) soya milk
2 salad onions, chopped
I tablespoon lemon juice
vegetable oil for frying

FOR THE COATING
2 tablespoons cornflour
5 tablespoons dried breadcrumbs, or soya nuts ground to a powder in a coffee mill

Remove the wrapping from the tempeh and put the whole block into a pan with enough water just to cover. Bring to the boil and simmer for 15 minutes, then drain well and mash roughly.

Heat the oil in a saucepan, add the onion, cover and cook for 7–10 minutes, until the onion is tender and lightly browned. Add the cornflour and garlic to the onion, stir over the heat for a few seconds, then pour in the soya milk and stir to make a thick sauce. Remove from the heat.

Add the tempeh, salad onions and lemon juice to the onion mixture. Season well with salt and pepper.

For the coating, mix the cornflour with 2–3 tablespoons of water to make a runny paste.

Shape the tempeh mixture into four burgers, dip each into the paste, then into the breadcrumbs or ground soya nuts, coating all sides.

Heat I cm (½ in) of vegetable oil in a frying pan, add the burgers and fry for 2–3 minutes on each side until browned and crisp. Drain on kitchen paper and serve at once.

NATURAL PROTEIN FOODS

SWEET AND SOUR SEITAN

This is a quick and easy dish, full of different flavours. The secret is to make sure you fry the seitan until it's really crisp before you stir-fry the vegetables. You could use other vegetarian protein foods, such as tofu, Quorn or TVP instead of the seitan.

serves 2–3

> 2 tablespoons vegetable oil
> 225 g (8 oz) seitan, cut into thin strips
> I red pepper, cut into strips
> 2 carrots, cut into strips
> I fat courgette, cut into strips
> I small pineapple, peeled and cut into strips,
>   or 450 g can of pineapple pieces in juice, drained
> bunch of salad onions, cut into strips
>
> **FOR THE SAUCE**
> I tablespoon fresh lemon juice
> I tablespoon cider vinegar
> I tablespoon soy sauce
> I tablespoon runny honey
> I tablespoon grated fresh ginger
> 2 garlic cloves, crushed

Heat the oil in a large saucepan or wok and fry the seitan until crisp. Remove the seitan from the pan, then add the vegetables and stir-fry for 3–4 minutes, or until the vegetables are still crisp but getting tender.

Meanwhile, mix all the sauce ingredients in a small bowl with some salt and pepper. Pour the sauce into the vegetables, stirring. Add the seitan and cook for a further minute or two, to get everything hot, then serve.

SOY SAUCE The soy sauce I love is tamari, which is traditionally processed and made without chemicals, sugar or preservatives, and is becoming much more widely available outside specialist shops.

GRILLED SEITAN WITH ONIONS

I do like this mixture of chewy seitan and sweet grilled onions; you can stop there, or you can go on to make the onions into a glorious rich gravy in which to serve the seitan. This would also work with Quorn or TVP pieces.

serves 2

225 g (8 oz) seitan
3 teaspoons rapeseed oil
225 g (8 oz) onion, quite finely sliced
1 teaspoon brown sugar
1 tablespoon flour
2 teaspoons vegetable bouillon powder
1 teaspoon Dijon mustard
1 teaspoon vegetarian Worcestershire sauce

Heat the grill. Drain, pat dry and slice the seitan quite thinly. Sprinkle with 1 teaspoon of the oil, mix with your fingers so all the seitan is coated, then spread it out on one side of a grill pan.

Sprinkle the sliced onion with another teaspoon of oil and the sugar. Mix thoroughly with your fingers and put on the other side of the grill pan.

Grill for about 15 minutes, stirring the pieces around from time to time – but don't mix the onion and seitan – until the onion is tender and both are tinged brown. You can mix them together and serve at this stage, if you wish, or keep the seitan warm under the grill while you make the onions into a gravy.

To make the gravy, heat the remaining teaspoon of oil in a saucepan, add the onions from the grill, and also add the flour to the pan. Stir over the heat for 1–2 minutes to brown the flour, then stir in 400 ml (14 fl oz) water, the bouillon powder, mustard and Worcestershire sauce. Simmer for 5 minutes, season to taste, then serve with the seitan, either separately or all mixed together.

VEGETARIAN WORCESTERSHIRE SAUCE This is available, for your cooking and your Bloody Marys, but you may have to seek it out. Standard Worcestershire sauce contains anchovy essence – if in doubt, read the label.

ASIAN-STYLE BRAISED TEMPEH ★

This is very tasty and nutritious. Serve it with quickly cooked Asian greens, such as pak choy or mustard greens, or spinach, and some transparent mung noodles or boiled basmati rice (if you're not slimming), for a more substantial meal.

Serves 2

225 g (8 oz) tempeh, quite thinly sliced
2 tablespoons rapeseed oil
1 tablespoon sesame oil
2 garlic cloves, sliced
1 teaspoon grated ginger
2 tablespoons soy sauce
2 tablespoons mirin
2 salad onions, chopped

Shallow-fry the tempeh in the rapeseed oil, turning it over when the first side is crisp and golden brown, then drain on kitchen paper. You'll probably need to do it in more than one batch.

When the tempeh is all done, discard any remaining oil from the frying pan, clean it with some kitchen paper and add the sesame oil. Heat, then add all the fried tempeh.

Sizzle for a minute, then add the garlic, ginger, soy sauce and mirin. Stir over the heat for a few more seconds, until the tempeh is bathed in a glossy brown sauce, then remove from the heat, scatter with the salad onions, and serve.

For an extra kick, you could add some chopped red chilli to the mixture when you put the tempeh into the sesame oil.

30-MINUTE DINNER PARTIES

TOFU AND ARAME SALAD ★

Sometimes I just fancy a clean-tasting salad with an oil-free Japanese dressing and a tang of the sea, and one day when I was in one of those moods, this is the salad I came up with. Arame (page 124) is a sea vegetable which can be found at good health food shops. You also need a really decent tofu, tender and delicate, to make this.

serves 2–4

25 g (I oz) arame
250 g packet of tofu, drained and blotted on kitchen paper
I tablespoon rice vinegar
I tablespoon soy sauce
few drops of umeboshi plum seasoning (see below) or lemon juice
½–I fresh, large (mild) red chilli, seeded and finely chopped
90 g packet fresh watercress

FOR THE SESAME SALT (GOMASHIO)
2 tablespoons sesame seeds
I teaspoon sea salt

Cover the arame with boiling water, soak for 5 minutes, then drain, rinse, chop and put into a bowl.

Cut the tofu into 5 mm (¼ in) cubes and put into the bowl with the arame, rice vinegar, soy sauce, umeboshi plum seasoning or lemon juice and the chilli, and stir together.

Heap the tofu mixture up on a serving dish or on individual plates, and arrange the watercress around the edge.

To make the gomashio, put the sesame seeds and salt into a dry saucepan and stir over the heat until the seeds smell and look toasted and start jumping around in the pan. Grind with a pestle and mortar or in a clean electric coffee mill, and serve with the salad.

UMEBOSHI PLUMS AND SEASONING Umeboshi is a variety of plum that has been pickled in salt. Its sharp, salty sweetness is very pleasant with Japanese dishes, even just plain cooked rice. You can buy the whole pickled plums, a purée and a liquid seasoning in a bottle. They're all quite pricey, but a little goes a long way and they keep for months in the fridge.

WESTERN-STYLE TEMPEH WITH MUSHROOMS

I like to use soya cream for this — it seems right to use it with a soya product, and it gives an excellent result. In fact I'd be surprised if anyone could tell the difference. But if you want to use single cream, please feel free, it will work just as well. Serve with a cooked green vegetable like slim green beans, or a green salad.

serves 2

225 g (8 oz) chestnut mushrooms, sliced
2 tablespoons olive oil
225 g (8 oz) tempeh, quite thinly sliced
2 garlic cloves, sliced
1 tablespoon arrowroot or kuzu (see below) or cornflour
250 ml (9 fl oz) soya cream (see page 169)
juice of ½ lemon
grated nutmeg
chopped parsley, to serve

Fry the mushrooms in 1 tablespoon of oil in a large sauté pan or wok for 4–5 minutes, or until they're tender, then remove them from the pan.

Heat the remaining oil in the pan and fry the tempeh on both sides until crisp and golden brown. You'll probably need to do it in more than one batch.

Add the mushrooms and garlic to the tempeh and stir-fry until everything is hot.

Mix the arrowroot, kuzu or cornflour with enough of the cream to make a paste. Add the rest of the cream to the tempeh mixture and bring to the boil, then pour in the paste and stir until thickened.

Add the lemon juice and salt, pepper and nutmeg to taste, then remove from the heat, scatter with chopped parsley and serve.

KUZU AND ARROWROOT These are both thickeners that are said to aid digestion. Kuzu looks like rough lumps of white chalk. Arrowroot is made from a root of that name and comes in the form of white powder. You can buy both at health food shops and some supermarkets. Arrowroot is cheaper than kuzu. They are used like, and interchangeably with, cornflour.

DEEP-FRIED TOFU AND HIJIKI BALLS

A delicious vegetarian taste of the sea that's packed with nutrients. These are great as a starter or with drinks, served with the soy and ginger dip. I must say I also like them with the Tartare Sauce on page 146. For more details on buying and using sea vegetables, see page 124.

makes 24

25 g (1 oz) hijiki seaweed
250 g packet of tofu, drained and blotted on kitchen paper
50 g (2 oz) grated carrot or turnip
1 garlic clove, crushed
2 teaspoons grated fresh ginger
3 tablespoons sesame seeds, or soya nuts ground in a coffee mill
vegetable oil

FOR THE DIP
2 tablespoons soy sauce
1 tablespoon apple juice concentrate
1 teaspoon grated raw ginger

Cover the hijiki with boiling water and soak for 10 minutes. Then drain, cover with fresh water and simmer for 20 minutes until tender. Drain and blot dry with kitchen paper.

Break up the tofu roughly and put it into a food processor with the hijiki, carrot or turnip, garlic and ginger and whizz until it's blended and holds together. Alternatively, chop the hijiki fairly finely, then mash it with the tofu and other ingredients. Season to taste.

Form the tofu mixture into walnut-sized balls and roll them in the sesame seeds or ground soya nuts. Make the dip by mixing together the soy sauce, mirin and ginger.

Fill a saucepan about a third full with vegetable oil and heat. When the oil is hot enough – it's ready when you throw in a sesame seed and it immediately rises to the top and starts to brown – add some of the tofu balls and fry for 3–4 minutes until they're golden brown and crisp. Drain on kitchen paper and repeat until they're all done. Serve with the dip.

FRUIT, SUGAR AND SPICE

IF, LIKE ME, YOU'RE NOT KEEN ON USING DAIRY PRODUCE – FOR HEALTH OR ANIMAL WELFARE REASONS – AND YOU ALSO HAVE RESERVATIONS ABOUT FLOUR AND SUGAR BECAUSE OF THEIR HIGH GLYCAEMIC INDEX RATING (SEE PAGES 10–11), THEN WHAT IS LEFT FOR SWEET TREATS? A SURPRISING AMOUNT, ACTUALLY, AS I HOPE THIS SECTION OF THE BOOK SHOWS. LUSCIOUS FRUITS, CAKES MADE FROM GROUND ALMONDS, OATS, RICE AND BARLEY FLOURS, AND LOW GLYCAEMIC SWEETENINGS, AS WELL AS GORGEOUS CREAMS AND TOPPINGS MADE FROM COCONUT AND SOYA CREAM.

CHOOSING A SWEETENER

The best way to get sweetness in the low-GI diet is undoubtedly to eat fruit, as nature intended. And the more you do that – really feast on it whenever you have the urge for something sweet – the less you will need additional sweeteners. However, there are times when a little more sweetness is needed, and if, like me, you prefer to use natural rather than artificial sweeteners, which are the best options?

Apple juice concentrate and raw organic honey (from beekeepers who leave some honey for their bees rather than taking it all and feeding them sugar) have low GI ratings and are fine in small quantities, even when you're losing weight.

Instead of sugar I used to use granulated fructose, which is made from corn, or agave syrup, extracted from cacti and 90 per cent fructose. However, it has now been found that although fructose has a low GI rating, when eaten with other foods with higher ratings, it takes on the higher rating too. So now I think you might as well just use sugar occasionally and be done with it.

Real brown sugars, such as rapadura, Valdivia and Barbados muscovado, do contain a few more minerals than white sugar but they are still sugars when all is said and done. Molasses, a thick sticky black syrup, is what's taken out of the cane when it is processed to make white sugar. It is a concentrated source of iron and other minerals and useful in small quantities.

Then there's stevia, an intensely sweet white powder made from a herb, Stevia rebaudiana. It's used in about 40 per cent of manufactured sweet products in Japan and readily available in most countries of the world – but not in the UK, because here it is illegal to sell it. The European Scientific Commission refused to approve it 'due to lack of information supporting the safety of the product'. An odd decision, since stevia has been grown, studied and used for centuries in many countries.

You can buy stevia from the US and because you need so little – a speck the size of a sesame seed is enough to sweeten a cup of tea – it's light to post. Try the Stevita Company, www.stevitastevia.com, or www.nowfoods.com. Because stevia is so concentrated, it is often mixed with a natural 'bulker' such as rice powder, which is fine. It does have a faintly aniseed flavour, which some people don't like, and although pure stevia is about 300 times sweeter than sugar, its sweetness is somehow gentler and subtler than that of sugar and takes a while to get used to, but it is well worth a try. Add it little by little, tasting carefully, until you get the right amount of sweetness.

MANGO AND PASSION FRUIT ★

Passion fruit often look rather wrinkled – that's perfectly normal.
The secret is to choose fruits that feel heavy.

serves 4

2–3 large ripe mangoes
8 passion fruit

Cut the mangoes down each side of the flat stone, as close as you can to the stone. Remove the peel, slice the flesh and lay the pieces in a shallow dish or plate.

Halve the passion fruit and scoop the pulp and seeds over the mango. Leave for at least 30 minutes before serving to allow the fragrant flavours to mingle.

ORANGES AND PASSION FRUIT The colours are similar, the flavours different, in this variation. Use 6 large oranges instead of the mangoes. Hold an orange over a bowl and, with a sharp knife, cut off the peel, removing the white pith as well, cutting round and round, as if you were trying to take the peel off in one long curl. Repeat for the remaining oranges. Then either slice the oranges into thin rounds, or cut the juicy segments away from the skin and pith. Cover with passion fruit pulp as above.

PERSIMMONS OR SHARON FRUIT If you can find these at just the right point of ripeness – that is, very ripe indeed without having gone too far – they're divine. Just peel, chop and serve as above.

LYCHEES, KIWIS AND GINGER

This is a very refreshing mixture that I love to eat after spicy dishes.
I tend, rather lazily, to use canned lychees, which I find fragrant and
delicious, but fresh ones would be even nicer, and lower GI, if you have
the patience to peel off the hard skins.

serves 4–6

2 × 400 g cans of lychees
4 kiwi fruits
4 lumps of preserved ginger from a jar
4 tablespoons ginger syrup or apple juice concentrate

Drain the lychees and rinse under the cold tap to remove the syrup. Put the lychees onto a serving platter.

Peel the kiwis and slice into thin rounds or segments. Chop the preserved ginger roughly. Add the kiwis
and ginger to the platter and pour over the ginger syrup or concentrate. Mix lightly and serve.

APRICOT AND ORANGE FOOL WITH PISTACHIOS

This is a lovely sweet fool. You do need to allow the apricots time to
soak, but then it's just a question of whizz and serve. It's essential to use
organic apricots for this recipe.

serves 4–6

250 g (9 oz) organic whole dried apricots (see page 168)
juice of 4 oranges
250 g (9 oz) firm or silken tofu, drained and broken into pieces
125 ml (4 fl oz) soya cream (see page 169)
6–8 cardamoms, pods discarded, seeds crushed (optional)
25 g (1 oz) pistachio nuts, shelled and chopped

Soak the apricots in the orange juice for several hours – overnight if possible. Then whiz to a purée.

Add the tofu, soya cream and crushed cardamoms, if using, and whiz again to make a smooth, thick
cream. Spoon into individual glasses and sprinkle with the nuts.

DRIED FRUIT COMPOTE ★

This is popular in the Middle East and there are lots of variations. You can use different mixtures of dried fruits – soak them in water or fruit juice, then cook them or leave them as they are. If you choose to cook them, you can add spices such as a piece of cinnamon stick, a little grated fresh ginger or some crushed cardamom pods. When the compote is done, you can add pieces of fresh fruit and flaked or whole blanched almonds, or crushed pistachios. You can also make an intensely iron-rich version by adding 1 tablespoon of blackstrap molasses to the soaking liquid – this is useful as a pick-me-up and for iron boosting (see page 23). This compote can be served as a snack, as a dessert, or for breakfast, with cream, soya cream or thick yogurt. Leave out the nuts if you're slimming.

serves 4

115 g (4 oz) each of organic dried figs, apricots or peaches, dates or sultanas, and prunes (about 450 g/1 lb in total of whatever mixture you fancy)
water, apple juice or orange juice, to cover
50 g (2 oz) almonds, flaked or blanched, or pistachios, shelled and chopped

Wash the fruit and put it into a bowl. Cover completely with water or fruit juice and leave to stand for several hours – 24 hours isn't too long as it just goes on getting better. Or you could soak the fruit for a few hours, then simmer it for 20–30 minutes until very tender. If you're doing this, I think it's best to use water rather than fruit juice for soaking.

Serve warm or cold with the nuts mixed in or scattered on top.

ORGANIC DRIED APRICOTS If you've never tasted organic dried apricots, which are a modest-looking, mousy brown, you've no idea of the treat in store for you. They have the most wonderful, sweet, brown-sugary flavour. Eat them straight out of the packet – they make a healthy treat for children. Use them in the compote above, in the Apricot and Orange Fool with Pistachios on page 166, or simply make them into a purée by soaking (or lightly cooking) in water, then puréeing. Spoon this over yogurt, spread on bread or eat as it is. And do try Hunza apricots, which look like pebbles in the bag, but taste divine if you cover them with water and soak for a few hours, then cook gently for 15–20 minutes, or until tender and the liquid is syrupy. Alternatively you could eat them just as they are.

MULLED WINE PEARS

A spicy version of an old favourite. They're delightful on their own, or with yogurt, soya cream (see below) or ice cream and maybe some fancy biscuits if you really want to push the boat out.

serves 6

6 firm dessert pears
85 g (3 oz) caster sugar
400 ml (14 fl oz) red wine
grated zest of 1 organic orange
2 star anise
few drops of red vegetable colouring (optional)
2 tablespoons preserved ginger in syrup, finely chopped

Peel the pears, leaving them whole and keeping the stalks. Put the sugar into a saucepan with the wine, orange zest, 400 ml (14 fl oz) water and star anise and heat gently until the sugar has dissolved, then bring to the boil.

Add the pears, cover and simmer gently for 30–40 minutes, or until the pears are tender right through to the centre. If they look a bit drab, enhance them with a few drops of vegetable colouring, if you like.

With a slotted spoon, transfer the pears from the pan to a serving dish. Add the ginger to the pan and boil vigorously until the liquid has reduced and looks shiny, then pour this over the pears. Make sure the pretty star anise are visible.

Serve at room temperature with a bowl of whipped cream, a jug of soya cream or a bowl of ice cream.

SOYA CREAM The soya cream that is widely available in the UK comes in a 280 ml vacuum pack, has the appearance and consistency of single cream and a creamy, slightly sweet flavour. You can use it in all the ways you would use single cream. If you want a thicker cream for spooning, simply put it into a small saucepan and boil gently, uncovered, until it has reduced by about half. Cool, then use as required – it's lovely with the Mulled Wine Pears (see above), for instance. For a sharper 'soured cream' version, simply stir in 1 teaspoon or so of lemon juice, which will thicken it even more and also add sharpness.

HONEY AND CINNAMON-ROASTED FIGS

In the summer there's nothing to beat warm, sun-ripened figs, and nothing to do to them except eat them. However, when you can't get them, here is a way to make less-than-perfect fresh figs really heavenly.

serves 4

12 figs
3 tablespoons clear honey
2–3 teaspoons cinnamon
thick Greek yogurt, to serve

Preheat the oven to 200°C/400°F/Gas Mark 6, or prepare a hot grill.

Cut a cross in the top of each fig, going through the stem but not right through the base, so that the pieces remain intact. Put them into a shallow casserole dish, pulling them open gently as you do. Drizzle the honey over the insides of the figs and sprinkle with cinnamon.

Bake, or grill, for about 15 minutes, until the figs are tender and fragrant but not collapsed. Serve with Greek yogurt.

HONEY AND CINNAMON-ROASTED PLUMS For this delicious variation, halve and stone 750 g (1 lb 10 oz) plums – it doesn't matter if they're hard. Put them into a casserole dish with the honey and cinnamon and cook as above, until tender.

FOR A VEGAN ALTERNATIVE, use agave syrup, brown rice syrup or apple juice concentrate instead of the honey.

EXOTIC FRUIT COMPOTE WITH COCONUT CREAM

If you can get fresh lychees, and have the time to peel off their hard
skin and take out the stones, then use them; otherwise, a can is fine.
Make sure all the fruit is ripe – buy it a few days in advance if necessary.

serves 4

2 tablespoons clear honey
juice of 2 oranges
I ripe mango
I paw paw
2 kiwi fruit
250 g (9 oz) black grapes
425 g can of lychees, drained
4 passion fruit

FOR THE COCONUT CREAM
200 g block of creamed coconut
grated zest of I lemon or lime
  or ½ teaspoon real vanilla extract (optional)
a little honey or apple juice concentrate

Start by making the coconut cream, so that it has time to cool. Cut the creamed coconut block into small pieces and put in a bowl set over a pan of steaming water. Add 6 tablespoons of boiling water to the coconut and leave for a few minutes to melt, then stir until smooth and creamy. Add the lemon or lime zest, or the vanilla extract (real vanilla tastes divine but darkens the cream slightly), and sweeten to taste – I find it sweet enough as it is. Leave to cool.

Make a fresh syrup by mixing the honey and orange juice in a large bowl.

Cut the mango down each side of the flat stone, as close as you can to the stone. Remove the peel, slice the flesh into chunks and add to the bowl.

Peel the paw paw, remove the seeds and slice the flesh. Peel and slice the kiwi fruit. Add these to the bowl, along with the grapes, halved and seeded if necessary, and the lychees.

Just before you want to serve the compote, halve the passion fruit, scoop out all the juice and seeds and add to the rest of the fruit. Stir gently, then serve with the cooled coconut cream.

FRUIT, SUGAR AND SPICE

PEACH AND BLUEBERRY COMPOTE ★

Another really simple recipe – but such a winner, in my opinion.
(And did you know that blueberries help retard the ageing process?)
The caster sugar is optional.

serves 4

4 peaches, washed, stoned and thinly sliced
500 g (1 lb 2 oz) blueberries, washed
4 tablespoons apple juice concentrate
4 tablespoons caster sugar (optional)

Put the peaches and blueberries into a saucepan with the apple juice concentrate and caster sugar, if using – it might not be necessary if the fruit is really sweet. Heat gently for 5–10 minutes, until the juices run and the peaches are just tender. Serve warm or cold.

VANILLA-POACHED PEACHES WITH ALMONDS Using 6–7 peaches instead of the peaches and blueberries, prepare the compote as above, adding 2 vanilla pods, broken in half. Cook until the peaches are tender, then add 3 tablespoons of whole blanched almonds.

BLACKBERRY AND APPLE COMPOTE Use 4 eating apples, peeled and sliced, and 500 g (1 lb 2 oz) blackberries instead of the peaches and blueberries. Put them into a pan with the apple juice concentrate and caster sugar, if using, and cook gently, with a lid on the pan, for 15–20 minutes, or until the apples are tender to the point of a knife. Serve warm or cold.

SUMMER BERRY COMPOTE Make as above, using 750 g (1 lb 10 oz) mixed summer berries: strawberries, redcurrants, blueberries, raspberries. Remove stalks and halve or quarter larger strawberries. Heat very gently with the apple juice concentrate and caster sugar, if using, until the juices run. If you're using redcurrants, you may need to add a bit more fructose or caster sugar.

SEASONAL CELEBRATIONS

YOGURT ICE CREAM WITH HONEY RASPBERRY SAUCE ★

I got the idea for this from one of Nigel Slater's recipes: banana and yogurt makes a smooth and creamy ice, which you can make sweeter with a drizzle of smoky maple syrup, some fragrant honey, or this honey and raspberry sauce. The ice cream is best made in an ice-cream maker.

serves 4

4 ripe and sweet bananas, peeled and roughly chopped
500 g plain unsweetened low-fat yogurt
for the sauce
250 g (9 oz) raspberries
4 tablespoons clear honey

Put the bananas in a food processor or blender with the yogurt and whiz until completely smooth.

Pour the mixture into an ice-cream maker, following the manufacturer's instructions, and freeze until very thick.

Meanwhile, make the sauce. Purée the raspberries and honey, then pass the mixture through a sieve to remove the seeds.

Serve the ice cream with the raspberry sauce.

SPICY APRICOT FLAPJACKS

Everyone loves these and they're so easy to make – and relatively
healthy too.

makes 20 pieces

> 125 ml (4 fl oz) olive oil
> 140 g (5 oz) light brown sugar
> 200 g (7 oz) rolled oats
> 50 g (2 oz) brazil nuts, chopped
> 50 g (2 oz) dried apricots, chopped
> ½ teaspoon ground ginger
> pinch of ground cinnamon
> 1–2 pinches of chilli flakes or powder
> 2 teaspoons water

Preheat the oven to 200°C/400°F/Gas Mark 6.

Simply mix all the ingredients together and press into a lightly oiled 19 x 29 cm (11 x 9 in) Swiss roll tin.
Bake for 10 minutes, until golden brown. Cool in the tin but mark into slices while the mixture is still
warm. The mixture is quite crumbly so don't try to get the flapjack pieces out of the tin until they're
completely cold, and use a spatula when you do.

FLAPJACK VARIATIONS You can vary the dried fruit and nuts used – chopped dried
peaches are good, as are raisins or sultanas. If you're making them for young children, you might like to
leave out the nuts or use sunflower, pumpkin or sesame seeds. Plain flapjacks, without either nuts or dried
fruit, also work well. For a particularly nutritious (but strong-tasting) version, replace the syrup with 1
tablespoon (or more) of blackstrap molasses.

FRUIT, SUGAR AND SPICE

SPARKLING RASPBERRY JELLY ★

This recipe makes a soft jelly you can easily get your spoon into. Prepare the jellies not more than an hour or so before you want to eat them and keep them in a cool place, but not the fridge, which can make them go dull-looking.

serves 4–6

750 ml (1¼ pints) white grape juice
8 teaspoons agar flakes or Vege Gel
140 g (5 oz) raspberries

Pour the grape juice into a saucepan. Sprinkle the agar flakes on top – don't stir – and heat gently for about 5 minutes, until the flakes have dissolved. Then bring to the boil, remove from the heat and set aside to cool briefly. If you are using Vege Gel, follow the packet instructions.

Meanwhile, divide the raspberries between 4–6 glass bowls or deep wine glasses. Pour the warm grape juice over the raspberries. Leave to cool, then chill in the fridge.

VEGETARIAN GELATINE This is made from a type of seaweed called agar. You can buy it in flakes from specialist health shops, or as Vege Gel from supermarkets. It does not behave like normal gelatine – for one thing, it sets very quickly indeed – and it has its limitations, but it will set any fruit juice to make a sparkling jelly.

STICKY PARKIN

This perennial favourite will keep in a tin for 7–10 days and it just goes on getting more and more gorgeously sticky.

makes 12–16 pieces

4 tablespoons olive oil
175 g (6 oz) black treacle or blackstrap molasses
8 tablespoons apple juice concentrate
115 g (4 oz) light brown sugar
115 g (4 oz) fine wholemeal flour
2 teaspoons baking powder
1 tablespoon ground ginger
115 g (4 oz) medium oatmeal
6 tablespoons soya milk

Preheat the oven to 160°C/325°F/Gas Mark 3. Line a 20 cm (8 in) square tin with non-stick baking parchment.

Put the olive oil, black treacle or blackstrap molasses (if you dip the spoon into the oil first, the molasses will slither off the spoon easily), apple juice concentrate and sugar into a saucepan and heat gently until melted.

Put the wholemeal flour, baking powder, ginger and oatmeal into a bowl. Stir the soya milk into the melted ingredients, which will cool them down, then pour on top of the dry ingredients and mix together quickly.

Pour the mixture into the prepared tin and bake for 50–60 minutes, or until it springs back when pressed lightly in the centre. Cool in the tin, then cut into pieces.

STICKY DATE BREAD

This is a dark, moist bread studded with sweet, gooey pieces of date.
Serve in thick slices, spread with a little butter if you like.

makes 1 loaf

> **2 tablespoons apple juice concentrate**
> **4 tablespoons black treacle or blackstrap molasses**
> **5 tablespoons soya milk**
> **4 tablespoons olive oil**
> **225 g (8 oz) barley flour or wholemeal flour**
> **1 teaspoon mixed spice**
> **1 teaspoon baking powder**
> **50 g (2 oz) light brown sugar**
> **115 g (4 oz) stoned and chopped dates**

Preheat the oven to 190°C/375°F/Gas Mark 5. Line a 450 g (1 lb) loaf tin with a long strip of non-stick (or greased greaseproof) paper over the base and up the narrow sides.

Heat the apple juice concentrate, black treacle or blackstrap molasses, and the soya milk gently in a saucepan until dissolved, then stir in the oil, remove from the heat and set aside.

Put the barley flour, mixed spice, baking powder, sugar and the dates into a bowl. Pour in the melted syrup mixture and stir until combined. Spoon into the prepared tin and bake for 50–60 minutes, or until the top is firm to a light touch and a skewer inserted into the centre comes out clean.

Cool in the tin, then turn out and peel off the paper.

LEMON CAKE

This is a beautiful moist golden cake with an intense lemon flavour.
It contains no flour and is perfect to serve with a berry or other fruit
compote (I particularly like it with the Summer Berry Compote on page
175), or to eat on its own. You really need an electric whisk to make this.

makes I cake

2 lemons, unwaxed, preferably organic
6 eggs
200 g (7 oz) caster sugar
250 g (9 oz) ground almonds

Preheat the oven to 150°C/300°F/Gas Mark 2. Line a 20 cm (8 in) round cake tin – preferably springform or with a loose base – with non-stick baking parchment.

Wash the lemons, then put them into a pan, cover with water and bring to the boil. Leave to cook gently for about 45 minutes, or until the lemons are very tender when tested with a sharp knife. Leave to cool.

Drain the lemons and cut them open so you can remove any pips. Then put the lemons into a food processor and whiz to a golden purée.

Whisk the eggs and sugar together for about 5 minutes until they are pale and very thick, and until a little of the mixture, flicked on top of the rest, will hold its shape for a few seconds.

Whisk in the lemon purée, then fold in the ground almonds using a metal spoon.

Pour the mixture into the tin, then bake for 1¼ hours, or until a cocktail stick inserted into the centre of the cake comes out clean. If it starts to get too brown, cover lightly with a piece of greaseproof paper. Cool the cake in the tin, then turn out carefully and remove the paper.

VEGAN VICTORIA SANDWICH CAKE

This is a delightful cake; the orange makes it a pretty pale gold colour, like a classic Victoria sandwich cake, and adds a delicate flavour which goes well with the raspberry jam. The consistency is light and moist – no one would guess there were no eggs in this cake unless you told them.

makes 1 cake

175 g (6 oz) organic white self-raising flour
3 teaspoons baking powder
85 g (3 oz) caster sugar
115 g (4 oz) ground almonds
grated zest of 1 orange
juice of 1 orange, made up to 300 ml ($\frac{1}{2}$ pint) with water
6 tablespoons olive oil

FOR THE FILLING AND TOPPING
2 tablespoons all-fruit raspberry jam
a little fructose or caster sugar, for sprinkling

Preheat the oven to 180°C/350°F/Gas Mark 4. Line the bases of 2 x 20 cm (8 in) sandwich tins with non-stick baking parchment.

Put the flour, baking powder, caster sugar, ground almonds and grated orange zest into a large bowl and mix, then add the orange juice and water mixture and the oil, and mix well.

Divide the mixture between the 2 tins and bake for 20 minutes, or until the tops of the cakes spring back when lightly pressed.

Leave to cool in the tins, then remove and strip off the paper. Sandwich the cakes together with the jam and sprinkle a little caster sugar on top of the cake.

CHOCOLATE VEGAN VICTORIA SANDWICH CAKE For this delectable variation, replace 50 g (2 oz) of the flour with the same quantity of good-quality cocoa powder. The grated orange zest is optional, but keep the juice as this helps the cake to rise. Sandwich the cakes with all-fruit black cherry jam, or a chocolate cream made by beating 85 g (3 oz) good-quality vegan margarine with 85 g (3 oz) icing sugar, 2 tablespoons of cocoa powder and 1 teaspoon of real vanilla extract, until light and fluffy. Dust the top of the cake with icing sugar.

CHOCOLATE MOUSSE CAKE

This is one of those chocolate cakes made without flour. Warm from the oven and still molten in the centre, this makes a perfect 'pudding cake' served for a special treat with a little chilled, lightly whipped cream, which blends voluptuously with the warm, oozing chocolate. When cold, it also makes a wonderful celebration cake, dense and gooey.

makes 1 cake

> **450 g (1 lb) dark chocolate**
> **115 g (4 oz) butter, cut into pieces**
> **6 free-range eggs**
> **115 g (4 oz) caster sugar**
> **1 tablespoon pure vanilla extract**
> **a little fructose or icing sugar to sprinkle (optional)**

Preheat the oven to 180°C/350°F/Gas Mark 4. Line a 20 cm (8 in) round cake tin – preferably springform or with a loose base – with non-stick baking parchment.

Break the chocolate into pieces and put into a heat-proof glass or china bowl with the butter. Set it over a pan of gently steaming water and leave to melt.

Meanwhile, separate the eggs. Whisk the whites until stiff. Leave on one side while you whisk together the yolks and sugar (no need to wash the whisk in between) until they're thick and pale.

Whisk the melted chocolate mixture in with the egg yolks, along with the vanilla extract, then, using a metal spoon, fold in the egg whites.

Tip the mixture into the prepared tin and bake for 25 minutes until set but still wobbly in the centre. If you want a firmer centre, cook it for 5–10 minutes longer. Cool in the tin. Remove the paper carefully before serving, and sprinkle over a little fructose or icing sugar, if using.

CHOCOLATE BROWNIES For chocolate brownies, make the cake as described, then bake it in a 23 x 33 cm (9 x 13 in) Swiss roll tin, lined with non-stick baking parchment, for 15–20 minutes, until just firm in the centre. Cool in the tin then cut into pieces. Tiny squares are lovely for a party or special dessert, each topped with a spoonful of cream, a strawberry and a dusting of icing sugar.

INDEX

Page numbers in *italic* refer to the illustrations

SOURCES

Apple juice concentrate Several good brands available from most health food shops; make sure you buy organic.

Apricots, organic, including Hunza apricots Available from good health food shops, Fresh and Wild and Planet Organic.

Blackstrap molasses You can find this in any health food shop.

Buckwheat Natural, untoasted buckwheat can be found in most health food shops.

Coconut flavouring From Jane Asher Party Cakes & Sugarcraft, 22–24 Cale Street, London SW3 3QU. Tel: +44 (0)20 7584 6177 www.jane-asher.co.uk

Creamed coconut, coconut milk Creamed coconut, in a solid block, and coconut milk, in cans, including organic varieties, are available from most supermarkets.

Curry leaves, fresh Available from any ethnic Indian shop, if you're lucky enough to live near one. Otherwise in packets, with the fresh herbs, in larger supermarkets.

Flours Doves Farm Fine Wholemeal Flour is available from most good health food shops and many supermarkets. Doves Farm also make a beautiful chick pea (gram) flour. Tel: +44 (0)1488 684 880, www.dovesfarm.co.uk. For oatmeal, barley or millet flour you'll need to go to a good health food shop.

Green soya beans (edamame) Buy these frozen from Chinese or Japanese shops; also frozen podded in health-food shops.

Linseeds or flax seeds Best to buy these whole, and grind them yourself. They are quite widely available from most health food shops.

Miso Organic whole barley miso is available from good health food shops.

Nut butters Lovely organic nut butters are available from health food shops. Rapunzel is a brand to look out for, particularly the white and the brown almond varieties. When buying peanut butter, make sure it's organic and free from both sugar and palm oil.

Sea vegetables and agar flakes Marketed by Clearspring and now available in some supermarkets and most good health food shops.

Seitan The plain, natural type is available from large, specialist health-food stores.

Soy sauce Kikkoman is available from any large supermarket. Tamari can be found at good health food shops; Clearspring make a lovely one.

Soya yoghurt, soya milk and soya cream Sojasun make a natural live organic soya yoghurt – buy it from good health food shops. Soya Dream (that is, soya cream) is available from health food shops and supermarkets.

Stevia To buy this from the US, try the Stevita Company, www.stevitastevia.com, or www.nowfoods.com.

Tahini Be sure to buy the light one as dark tahini is rather bitter. Available from good-quality health food shops and Cypriot or Greek shops.

Tempeh Try to find Dragonfly tempeh, which is pale and delicate, or the one made by Impulse Foods. Available from specialist health-food shops.

Tofu Dragonfly tofu is firm but light and delicate, too. You can buy it from specialist health-food shops.

Transparent noodles The best place to get these cheaply is a Chinese or Japanese supermarket, but you probably won't be able to read the packet. The Montignac Food Boutique and Café stocks pasta made from mung beans.

Unrefined salt You can buy this in any supermarket in Brittany or at the Montignac Food Boutique and Café. Tel: +44 (0)20 7370 2010, www.montignac.co.uk It can also be obtained from Villandry. Tel: +44 (0)20 7631 3131, www.villandry.com

OMEGA-3 SUPPLEMENTS

Superfood, a wonderful nutritional supplement made from completely natural ingredients and packed with vitamins and, importantly, vegetarian sources of long-chain omega-3 oils. Available from Herbs Hands Healing Ltd, tel: +44 (0)845 345 3727, www.herbshandshealing.co.uk

DHA Gold capsules Available from supermarkets and pharmacies. www.dhadepot.com

Neuromins capsules Available from supermarkets and pharmacies. www.martekbio.com

www.roseelliot.com